DEFENCE COMMITTEE

Ninth Report

MILITARY TRAINING

Report, together with the
Proceedings of the Committee
relating to the Report,
Minutes of Evidence and
Memoranda

Ordered by The House of Commons *to be printed*
29 September 1994

LONDON: HMSO

£17.00 net

93
[Including 810 of Session 1992-93]

The Defence Committee is appointed under Standing Order No 130 to examine the expenditure, administration and policy of the Ministry of Defence and associated public bodies.

The Committee consists of 11 Members, of whom the quorum is three. Unless the House otherwise orders, all Members nominated to the Committee continue to be members of it for the remainder of the Parliament.

The Committee has power:

(a) to send for persons, papers and records, to sit notwithstanding any adjournment of the House, to adjourn from place to place, and to report from time to time;

(b) to appoint specialist advisers either to supply information which is not readily available or to elucidate matters of complexity within the Committee's order of reference;

(c) to communicate to any other committee appointed under the same Standing Order (or to the Committee of Public Accounts) its evidence and any other documents relating to matters of common interest;

(d) to meet concurrently with any other such committee for the purposes of deliberating, taking evidence, or considering draft reports.

MONDAY 13 JULY 1992

The following were nominated Members of the Committee:

Sir Nicholas Bonsor
Mr Menzies Campbell
Mr Churchill
Mr Michael Colvin
Mr Frank Cook
Sir Nicholas Fairbairn

Mr Bruce George
Mr John Home Robertson
Mr John McWilliam
Mr Neville Trotter
Mr Peter Viggers

Sir Nicholas Bonsor was elected Chairman on 15 July 1992.

The cost of printing and publishing this Report is estimated by HMSO at £13,218.
The cost of preparing for publication the shorthand minutes of evidence taken before the Committee and published with this Report was £762.08.

TABLE OF CONTENTS

NINTH REPORT

The Defence Committee has agreed to the following Report:

MILITARY TRAINING

I INTRODUCTION

1. Military training in all three Services absorbs a significant share of the total defence budget, and has been subject to considerable change over the past few years, primarily but not exclusively because of the Options for Change process of drawdown. Fewer initial entrants as a result of falling Service manpower numbers, growing pressures to reduce the training system's costs and land usage, increasing constraints on training and exercising as a result of public pressure, and international political developments have combined to produce substantial changes. We therefore decided in 1993 to inquire into various matters connected with training in each of the three Services, including "continuation" training in the form of exercises. In the course of the inquiry, we began a separate inquiry into aspects of the MoD Estate: some of the information we have assembled on training lands will be covered in the Report on that subject.

2. On 14 July 1994 the Secretary of State announced the outcome of the Defence Costs Study, with the publication of the Front Line First document (FLF) and a separate announcement of various enhancements. One of the studies was into training, and several of the enhancements provided by savings over and above those required by the PES 93 settlement are to be devoted to improved training. However, no separate document on training was published. The principal proposals, covering the proposed establishment in 1997 of a Joint Services Command and Staff College, and changes to the flying training system, were covered in 10 brief paragraphs of FLF. FLF also stated that further studies into specialist training would be conducted. Both the Army and the Royal Navy are engaged in further reviews of training. The Army review "which is separate from but consistent with the defence costs study" will cover the nature and content of training courses generally as well as specified areas including adventurous training, catering training and market testing, to which we refer below.[1] FLF refers baldly to "further rationalisation and streamlining" being planned.[2] It also records that "a major review of Royal Navy training is due to report in the autumn".[3] We regret that the full DCS report on training was not published, and look to MoD to ensure that proposals emerging from the two single Service studies are fully aired. **It is evident that training in all three Services is in a state of almost continuous review, which may not always be conducive to an effective outcome.**

3. The Committee heard oral evidence from the Director General Army Training and others on 7 July 1993: from the Director General Naval Manpower and Training and others on 8 December 1993: and from the Assistant Chief of the Air Staff, the then Air Officer Training (now Chief Executive RAF Training Group Defence Agency) and others on 23 March 1994. We paid useful visits to a number of Royal Navy (RN) Training Establishments in the Portsmouth area in October 1993 and to the Royal Military College of Science at Shrivenham in June 1994. We had planned a September 1994 visit to the British Army Training Unit at Suffield in Alberta, Canada (BATUS), which has had to be postponed. We have also taken the opportunity of other informal visits to units in the UK and abroad over the past two years to inquire about training matters. In the course of our visit to Cyprus in May 1993, for example, we attended a Royal Marine Commando exercise in the Akamas Training Area in the north west of the island: and in June 1993 we saw in detail amphibious engineering training arrangements at Hameln in Germany. We express our thanks to all who have assisted us in these inquiries and visits.

---

[1] HC Deb, 7 July 1994, col 263*w*
[2] FLF, para 226
[3] *ibid*

4. The interest of this Committee and its predecessors in military training goes back some way. In the 1970s our predecessors on the Defence and External Affairs Sub-Committee of the Expenditure Committee undertook several inquiries into training, and in particular on the scope for more tri-Service training to be conducted. In Session 1980-81 our predecessors on the Defence Committee undertook an inquiry into RAF Pilot Training in the light of the serious shortage of pilots for fast jet flying:[4] the evidence taken at that time has proved most useful in looking at current practice. Although there have been no Reports since then specifically directed at training, the subject has been touched on in a number of other inquiries. We propose to monitor a number of the developments referred to below, and those arising from the reviews currently underway, in the course of our annual inquiries into the Statement on the Defence Estimates.

II MANAGEMENT AND ORGANISATION

Central administration

5. **All three Services are in the midst of a reorganisation of the way in which both initial and in-service training is managed, generally working towards a common pattern of an Agency reporting to the 4-star personnel Top Level Budget holder.**

—The RN has brought together in one new Command based at Portsmouth the former Second Sea Lord's personnel responsibilities, and the Chief of Naval Home Command's responsibilities. Within that Command, the RN's flag officer training and recruiting (FOTR) organisation, employing around 3,900 Service personnel and 1,500 civilians, is now a potential candidate for Agency status.[5]

—The Army has formed a 3-star Inspectorate General of Doctrine and Training (IGDT) at Upavon in Wiltshire, currently under CinC UKLF, but apparently to be transferred to the Adjutant General, employing around 18,000 service and civilian personnel and with a budget of around £525 million.[6] Agency status for IGDT is being considered.[7]

—The RAF Training Group Defence Agency was established on 1 April 1994, under the newly formed Personnel and Training Command, with a budget of some £315 million, and employing around 6,000 Service and 2,500 civilian personnel. This is expected to produce a more business-like stance, and give greater freedom to station commanders, as well as greater flexibility in financial management, including the generation of income.[8] Originally expected to have been among the earliest MoD agencies, its establishment has been delayed by difficulties in establishing policy responsibility: it is now clear that the Chief Executive has broad policy as well as day-to-day administrative responsibilities.[9]

6. It can be seen that the three Services are all proceeding along broadly the same path, and one which we welcome. There are however several distinctive features:

—While the Royal Military Academy Sandhurst, the Staff College at Camberley and the Royal Military College of Science at Shrivenham are Basic Level Budget Holders within IGDT, the RAF College Cranwell and the Staff College at Bracknell, although subordinate to the 4-star officer commanding the Personnel and Training Command, are not within the new RAF Training Agency: a matter which the Committee was told was being looked at under the Defence Costs Study, but on which nothing appears in FLF.[10]

---

[4]First Report, HC 53 of Session 1980-81

[5]Q281; SDE 94, para 542 and HC Deb, 23 June 1994, col 249w

[6]Evidence, p 39, A1; *ibid*, p 44, A1

[7]SDE 94, para 542; FLF, para 226

[8]Qq 1339ff; 1994 Corporate Plan

[9]Q1341; SDE 91 Report, HC 394 of Session 1990-91, Evidence, p 59, A14

[10]Q1348; Evidence, p 45, A1

—The extent to which Service doctrine and in-service training is integrated into the main training structure varies between the Services. Only the Army would seem to have whole-heartedly followed the American template of Training and Doctrine Commands. The RN maintains a separate Flag Officer Sea Training. The RAF formed a free-standing Air Warfare Centre (AWC) in October 1993, bringing together a number of existing units under a one-star commander at RAF Waddington. The AWC, the formation of which was one of the key lessons of the Gulf War,[11] is intended to provide a "centre of excellence" in operational doctrine and training, with an important training function at the higher command level.

—Practice also varies on the extent to which training expenditure is controlled from within an identifiable training budget. Operational commanders by and large retain the control of training and exercising of forces under their command. In the Army, for example, much Field Army activity, in practice "continuation" training, comes out of other budgets, as do the substantial costs of training facilities maintained abroad, notably BATUS. Flying training for in-service aircrew is not within the responsibility of the RAF Training Group Defence Agency.

While there is no good reason to expect the different circumstances in the three Services to produce identical administrative solutions, we consider that there would be much to be gained if comparisons were made between the different approaches to similar issues. No doubt some such comparisons were made in the Defence Costs Study: they deserve publication.

Tri-Service training

7. The principal focus of the Expenditure Committee inquiries in the 1970s was the extent of tri-Service training, a matter also pursued in detail by the NAO in a 1987 Report. Although the Defence Training Committee (DTC) continues in being, and despite additions to the paper mountains of studies by the individual Services and various departmental Committees,[12] **there has not been any discernible movement towards more joint training.** We were told in oral evidence that a new joint *diving* school was to be established:[13] the NAO Report records that a DTC working party recommended co-location of the Army and RN diving schools at HMS Vernon in July 1983. After endless studies, there is now a Joint Services Animal Centre for *dog* training. There have also been advances in the volume of Fleet Air Arm flying training carried out for the RN at RAF establishments. But it was recently judged inappropriate to organise aero-engineering training at a joint service establishment on the closure of HMS Daedalus at Lee-on-Solent, despite the growing commonality of aircraft and helicopter types between the Services. The proposal arising from the Defence Costs Study for a tri-Service Defence Helicopter Flying School at least represents a step forward: and the options under consideration for various forms of specialist training are to include the possibility of lead Service or tri-Service training.[14] We refer below to the proposal for a Joint Services Command and Staff College, at either Greenwich or Camberley, with two-thirds of the course to be truly joint, and with the continuing single Service junior courses to be collocated.

8. By far the most expensive joint training establishment at the time of the 1987 NAO Report was the Army Catering Corps Training Centre. The DTC in 1973 endorsed separate Service training for cooks because of different training objectives: but in 1976 recommended centralisation at Aldershot, and validated the costs of this in 1978. In 1983-84 the RN and RAF moved to Aldershot. **We discovered in the course of our inquiry that both Services have now decided to return to previous arrangements.** The RN is to construct a new building at the RN Supply School at HMS Raleigh in Plymouth for the purpose, and the RAF

---

[11]Qq 1335-7

[12]NAO Report on Individual Training in the Armed Services, HC 212 of Session 1986-87, Appendix 4

[13]Q417

[14]FLF, para 326; para 330 and Figure 9. For current facilities for helicopter flying training at Middle Wallop and Shawbury, see DCS Report, Evidence, p41, A8

is to provide catering training at RAF Halton.[15] The premises hitherto used at Aldershot are to close. Investment appraisals showed that it would be cheaper to return to single Service training. The RN told us that there had been an excessive wastage rate among their cooks at Aldershot, of up to half in some years, and that they had had the additional expense of running a "naval administration" there.[16] The schools had never really merged; MoD described the Aldershot centre in evidence as "merely a home for three collocated schools rather than one combined school".[17] **It may well be that the death of the unsung flagship of tri-Service training establishments will not be widely mourned; but the fate of an insufficiently integrated establishment should act as a warning to those contemplating similar steps for training staff officers, helicopter pilots, musicians and others.**

9. While we accept that there are occasional efforts devoted centrally to seeking sensible arrangements for tri-Service or lead Service training, we have the firm impression that there is a tendency to seek synergy within a Service rather than to seek it outside. The financial savings expected to flow from concentration on fewer standard equipments across all three Services would be increased were tri-Service training to be seen as the first and not the last resort. **We welcome the renewed impetus towards joint Service training given by the Defence Costs Study.**

Civilianisation

10. **The numbers and proportion of relatively expensive Service personnel in the training system remain high.** The RAF has, for example, over 1,000 qualified flying instructors, qualified weapons instructors and other aircrew instructors, representing a substantial proportion of qualified aircrew.[18] 72 per cent of the RAF's Training Group Defence Agency are Service personnel, exactly the same figure as for the RN's FOTR. We note that there are 129 Service personnel on the staff of BRNC Dartmouth, including 50 officers, compared to around 170 civilian personnel.[19] From the trend in staff numbers shown in the RAF Training Agency's plans, the numbers of both Service and civilian personnel to be employed are to fall substantially over the next five years, but retaining around 4,000 Service personnel into the next century.[20] The principal justification for this is that it ensures that those receiving initial and in-service training are instructed by those with the most recent experience and expertise; the use of Service personnel provides the essential element of credibility, particularly necessary on in-service courses. On our visit to RMCS Shrivenham, we saw how a relatively small number of highly able officers in mid-career were able to inject a valuable note of realism into technical staff education of young officers. **The scope for further civilianisation of military training is evidently considerable: but the recent experience and professional credibility which only Service personnel can give must be retained, as well as the capability to reconstitute forces using the pool of qualified personnel in the training system, and the possibility of offering some career advancement to those with specialist skills who do not wish to be promoted to a staff or desk job.**

Contractorisation and market testing

11. The Service training organisations have varied in the extent to which they have pursued contractorisation and market testing. For a number of years, the RAF has let multi-activity contracts covering Engineering and Supply, and now domestic support, at its training stations at Cranwell, Finningley, Linton-on-Ouse and Shawbury. In 1993 it let a new multi-activity contract at Scampton.[21] It also let an elementary flying contract at Topcliffe in July 1993,

---

[15] Qq 417ff; Qq 1349-50

[16] Q419; Evidence, pp 62-64, A13e

[17] *ibid*, p 63, A13e(iii)

[18] HC Deb, 14 June 1994, cols 529-530

[19] HC Deb, 26 May 1994, col 230w

[20] For recent Written Answer on the use of contractorised Skyvan aircraft in place of RAF balloons for parachute training and loss of 78 Service posts, see HC Deb, 13 July 1994, col 633w

[21] Similar contracts were let at Church Fenton and Swinderby, now closed: Evidence, p 65, A3 and p 69, Annex G. Scampton and Finningley are due to close in 1996-97: FLF, para 327

providing for elementary flying training to be conducted by a contractor using Firefly aircraft. Including those contracts now terminated on closure, the annual value of contracts let amounts to £31 million, producing a saving of around 2,500 Service and civilian posts.[22] The Agency's 10-year plan, based on LTC figures, anticipates almost doubling the cash costs of contractors, from £38 million to £72 million, within a static cash budget. The RN and Army seem to have been slower in identifying possible areas for market testing: of the 36 areas throughout MoD market tested in 1992 and 1993, none relate to RN or Army training.[23] The DCS announcement included plans to market test the majority of the Royal Armoured Corps (RAC) training regiment task, currently carried out by an RAC armoured regiment, as well as increasing the number of civilian flying instructors for Elementary and Basic flying training.[24] Private sector involvement in multi-engine training is to be sought.[25] **It is evident that military training in all Services offers some candidates ripe for market testing.**

Rationalisation and reconstitution

12. All three Services have undertaken a rationalisation of the number of their training establishments and of their system of training generally along lines long contemplated and discussed, for which the Options drawdown has provided the necessary impetus.

13. The *RN* plans to have reduced to 11 training establishments by 1998, following recent decisions to close HMS Daedalus and HMS Mercury.[26] Operational Sea Training is in the process of being moved from Portland to Devonport. The decision to move Flag Officer Sea Training (FOST) operations from Portland to Devonport was a controversial one, and we received a number of submissions drawing attention to problems which it was anticipated would arise. Foreign navies also use FOST's services, in return for their provision of SSKs to act as enemies there and elsewhere, under the Portland Credit Scheme which has been run since 1976.[27] Whatever the merits of the decision to move, we sought reassurance that the much admired service provided at Portland of bringing ships and their crews up to specified high standards, through carefully organised periods of various kinds of Operational Sea Training (OST), would not be affected by the move.   The Director Naval Manpower and Training assured us that the move was proceeding well, and that the throughput of ships would be the same as would have been achieved if sea training had remained at Portland.[28]

14. A number of changes to the previous pattern of operational sea training (OST) are being made as a result of the move. Basic OST will still last six weeks, but with reduced harbour time, and COST will be replaced by DOST (pre-deployment training), a new three weeks training package for ships entering the highest readiness categories. Time and money will be saved, and scarce assets made available for other purposes, by the use of contractorised civilian helicopters in place of Sea Kings for ferrying assessment and instructional staff to and fro. ASW Sea King support will be available from RNAS Culdrose, with fixed wing aviation support provided broadly as in the past. Proposals are still being considered for a new naval gunfire support training area, requiring the use of Dodman Point, and with new sea exercise areas for anti-air and anti-surface firings.[29] There has been local concern about the impact on fishermen. An announcement was made in May 1994 of a new twice daily information broadcast service to advise fishermen and other mariners of gun and missile firings in designated exercise areas around the UK, to be known as GUNFACTS, following the introduction of a similar service in relation to submarine operations.[30] **While some**

---

[22]*ibid*

[23]Sixth Report, HC 68 of Session 1993-94, Evidence, pp 42-45

[24]FLF, para 325; DCS Report, Evidence, p50, A26

[25]*ibid*, para 327

[26]Q281

[27]Qq 386ff, 399-401; Evidence, p 60, para e and Annex

[28]Q398

[29]Evidence, p 60, para c(iii); Q391; HC Deb, 20 June 1994, col 62*w*

[30]HC Deb, 26 May 1994, cols 233-4*w*

significant decisions remain to be taken on the implementation of the move of Sea Training from Portland to Plymouth, and while it seems to us inevitable that some of the concentration on the task which a base exclusively dedicated to training was able to achieve will be lost, it would seem that the move to Devonport is at least proceeding without evident problems.

15. The *RAF* is in the process of reducing its principal ground training stations to three, concentrating on Halton in Buckinghamshire for administrative training, Cosford in Shropshire for technical training and Locking in Avon for telecommunications training, with a further study into the "rationalisation" of Locking:[31] and the process of reducing its flying training stations continues apace.

16. The *Army* has concentrated initial recruit training at five basic training centres (Bassingbourn, Glencorse, Lichfield, Pirbright and Winchester), where all recruits receive a common basic 10-week military training.[32] This marks a radical departure from the previous system by which each Corps trained its own entrants at a large number of establishments. Despite misgivings among some as to the feasibility of throwing together recruits to, for example, the Guards Division and the former Army Catering Corps, now the Royal Logistic Corps, at Pirbright, the home of "spit and polish", the Director General Army Training told us that the outcome was at least as good if not better than under the previous system.[33] As a parallel process, a complex reorganisation of Phase 2 training is being implemented, including the transfer of Royal Artillery training from its historic home at Woolwich to Larkhill, of Royal Signals training from Catterick to Blandford, and the concentration in the long term of Phase 2 infantry training at Catterick.[34] Apprentice and technical training is also to be concentrated at Arms and Service centres.[35] While the drawdown in the Army and the creation of new Corps provided the opportunity for this major reorganisation, the plans in general reflect long-laid plans for rejigging the Army's organisation of initial training.

17. **We welcome the drive towards rationalisation of the number of training establishments. We are however concerned that, in the drive for economy, the practicalities of any required reconstitution of forces may be neglected.** We were disturbed to hear from the Chief of Staff, Naval Home Command, that —

> "...our major aim is to fix whatever the steady state level of recruitment ought to be and then adjust the complements and facilities and amenities in those establishments to match precisely that level"[36]

and to learn from the Director General Army Training in July 1993 that even the small rise in annual Army recruitment consequent on the Secretary of State's February 1993 "addback" of 3,000 — from 15,000 to around 15,700 — would produce some problems with accommodation.[37] There does seem to be some small reserve capacity designed into the RAF training system, described in evidence to us as "an element of headroom to cater for the unexpected". This has permitted it to train overseas personnel;[38] the Chief Executive of the Training Agency is evidently keen "to maximise income by marketing unavoidable spare capacity", seeking the freedom to negotiate the level of charges, which may be below what the Treasury suggests.[39] The Staff Colleges have long made places available for personnel from allied forces, but are obliged by Treasury rules to charge fees which go far beyond marginal cost. We heard how this has been one factor in reducing the Australian and

---

[31] Evidence, p 66, A5

[32] See Cm 1595, para 33; First Report, HC 218 of Session 1992-93, Evidence, p 60, 23

[33] Q2153; for significance of "capbadge integrity" to recruits, see Q2168

[34] SDE 93, para 716; Evidence, p 45, A2 on Crickhowell; OR, 16 December 1992, cols 335-6w; *ibid*, 22 July 1993, cols 351-2w

[35] Q2159

[36] Qq 277-8

[37] Qq 2160ff; Evidence, p 45, A3

[38] Qq 1323-5

[39] Evidence, p 75, A5; Q1330

Canadian presence at Shrivenham. We are relieved to see reference in FLF to continuing capacity for officers from overseas in the proposed Joint Services Command and Staff College.[40] **We are aware of the considerable value to British industry of being able to offer training in the UK for overseas forces personnel. The parameters of the military training system should not be drawn solely with currently planned force levels in mind, but should allow of at least a small margin for expansion, which could conveniently be used for training Service personnel from overseas and others as appropriate.**

III INDIVIDUAL TRAINING

Reduced recruitment

18. One of the challenges confronting the Services in the period of drawdown has been the reduction in throughput of new recruits, particularly in the RN and RAF: the Army has chosen to seek a higher proportion of redundancies as a means of continuing recruitment, albeit at a lower level. The RN training system has in addition suffered from a backlog in some branches resulting from past recruitment policies,[41] while in other branches there has been a recruitment freeze, exacerbated by a reduction in available berths as a result of cuts in the number of RN ships. MoD told us that as of January 1994 99 WE artificers were waiting for their first sea draft — ie their first posting at sea following extensive shore training — for an *average* of 12 months, with numbers from other Branches similarly stranded.[42] This bulge of young artificers awaiting their first ship should gradually be worked out:[43] but it is obviously a matter of concern that there should have been this mismatch. At the same time, RN training establishments are running at far below normal capacity, as we saw on our visits in October 1993: much useful effort is being devoted by Instructors to redesigning courses and in several cases towards rethinking the nature of the training to be provided and the output required.[44] In the RAF, recruit intakes into ground training have fallen dramatically from around 6,000 annually to under 1,000, and are not expected to recover to a "steady state" assumption of 5,750 until 1999; the Defence Costs Study and market testing is likely to produce a significant fall in this figure.[45] The numbers for basic trade training and further training have also fallen, albeit less sharply.[46] Pilot training numbers have also fallen, with only 70 to be brought into training in 1994/95 and 116 in 1995/96, compared to a target of 208 from 1996/97 onwards, and 305 in 1990/91.[47] **Whatever the outcome of the pilot project into the use of Job Centres for recruitment, the Royal Navy and the Royal Air Force face a major challenge in seeking to resume pre-contraction levels of recruitment.**

Single Entry

19. The Army seems to have been taken somewhat by surprise by the planned introduction in 1993 of the single school leaving point and consequent abolition of Junior Leader entry.[48] The Mountford Study estimated that around 800 to 1,000 recruits under 16 years 9½ months would be accepted each year, around 8 per cent of the total. By January 1994, 260 16 year olds had already been selected for recruit training by Recruit Selection Centres. A number of necessary steps to protect 16 and 17 year olds are being taken, including a degree of physical separation from trained soldiers, the provision of non-alcoholic recreation facilities,

---

[40]FLF, para 320

[41]For previous Committee critique of these, see Eighth Report, HC 637 of Session 1992-93, paras 50-55

[42]Evidence, pp 53-4, A1

[43]Qq 283-5

[44]Q276

[45]Evidence, p 69, Annex E

[46]*ibid*, Annex F

[47]*ibid*, pp 67-8, Annexes B and C

[48]Qq 2154-7

and an enhancement of the auxiliary welfare agencies.[49] **We regret the abolition of Junior Leader entry: and look forward to receiving details of the results of the review of Single Entry to the Army.**

Graduates

20. There has been a shift in all three Services towards a higher proportion of graduate officer entry, requiring changes to the length and content of the courses at Sandhurst, Cranwell and Dartmouth. At Sandhurst, the separate commissioning course for graduates and school leavers have been elided into a common commissioning course, the first of which began in September 1992 with a class over 80 per cent of whom were graduates.[50] Dartmouth's target of up to 70 per cent graduate entry has already been exceeded. While the training remains broadly as before, the shift towards a predominantly graduate entry is bound to have some effect.[51] The course at Cranwell has been lengthened.[52] The Director General Army Training also drew attention to the perceived "deficiencies in the instinctive leadership qualities of young people joining the Army over the last few years",[53] which had required an increasing emphasis on developing leadership skills during commissioning training, at the expense of purely low level military and infantry skills. The Royal Navy's major study into the Officer Corps, known from its principal author as the Layard Study, which proposed the introduction of an Initial Commission of 8-12 years, followed by Career Commissions, also proposed a minimum two A levels and three GCSEs for officer entry in place of the less ambitious five GCSEs.[54] **All three Services may have to adapt further if they are to seek to attract a yet higher proportion of graduate officer entry. We are not convinced that the long-term implications for officer training of an overwhelming graduate officer entry have been fully worked through by all Services.**

Manadon

21. The major recent change in officer training has been the decision to terminate the B.Eng course at the Royal Naval Engineering College (RNEC) at Manadon in Plymouth, which has led more or less inexorably to the closure of the College. The decision was founded on a fall from 90 to 60 in the annually required intake of Engineer Officers into the RN, of whom half are already recruited from graduates of "civilian" universities.[55] Retention of Manadon for the remaining 30 entrants a year would not be cost-effective, even if a range of other functions were moved there.[56] The alternative course of amalgamating RN engineer officer training with that provided at Shrivenham for officers of the two other services was regrettably not pursued. Instead, arrangements have been made with Southampton University for a sponsored course for an intake of 30 students each year. The sponsored students are to receive a bursary of £1,200 a year in addition to any DES or local authority grant or loan, reimbursable by those who do not subsequently enter the Service.[57] Manadon had hitherto offered a valued route for those from the "lower deck" — non-officers — with appropriate technical qualifications to undertake a degree course under the Upper Yardman scheme: for these to qualify for Southampton they will have to pass the same test as other students, without any assistance.[58] **In view of the wider significance of the Upper Yardman Scheme, we look to the Royal Navy to ensure that a proportion of its sponsored engineering students at the Southampton unit are drawn from the lower deck, providing**

---

[49]Evidence, p 50, A1(i)

[50]Evidence, p 45, A4; Qq 2169ff

[51]Qq 293-295, 329

[52]Q1345

[53]Q2172

[54]See Evidence, p 61, A13a

[55]Q323

[56]Evidence, pp 61-2, A13b and Qq 336-7

[57]Qq 310ff, 325-8

[58]Q306; Evidence, p 55, A3

so far as practicable equivalent opportunities for those hitherto offered by the Upper Yardman Scheme.

22. We received a number of submissions on the proposals to close RNEC Manadon. The proposal to establish a sponsored course at Southampton University with a Naval unit attached, and the status of students thereon as honorary RNR officers, will not satisfy the widespread sense that an opportunity has been lost to increase and concentrate the RN's resources in naval technological education rather than reducing and dispersing them. The Frodsham Report suggested an increase in Seaman Officers taking Manadon degrees, and recommended that Manadon —

"should evolve towards a more broadly based scientific and engineering centre for the Navy. The small Navy still needs an excellent technological training centre, but it cannot afford a proliferation of them".[59]

To this end, the Report endorsed the suggestions made by others, as far back as the Howard English Report of 1966, that the Department of Nuclear Science and Technology (DNST) should be transferred from Greenwich to Manadon, together with its associated JASON low power training reactor: and the Royal Corps of Naval Constructors first degree course. None of this will now be possible. It is possible that the RN's DNST will move to either SULTAN or to RMCS Shrivenham, and that the RN will look to either a civilian university or the commercial sector for reactor training facilities.[60] **We regret the closure of Manadon: and even more the loss of the opportunity for a tri-Service Engineering College at Shrivenham.**

Shrivenham

23. The DCS training study proposed that —

"we should build on Shrivenham's success and that it should be developed as the Defence Centre for science, technology and related management and finance training".[61]

We warmly welcome this proposal. As we saw on our visit to Shrivenham, it is a vibrant and forward-looking institution, with a well-established partnership with the civilian higher education sector. It is well placed to expand into less exclusively defence-related spheres, and has indeed already done so on IT management. **We await with interest publication of the outcome of the further consideration to be given to the proposal for further development of Shrivenham.**

Pilot training

24. There have been some significant changes since our predecessors reported on pilot training in 1980:

—the introduction of computer-based testing, probability scores, and the move (at greater cost and fewer receipts than anticipated) of the Officer Aircrew Selection Centre from Biggin Hill to Cranwell;[62]

—the introduction of a short Chipmunk Elementary Flying Training course to enable all entrants to progress to the shorter Tucano Basic Flying Training course;

—the creation of the joint RAF/RN Elementary Flying Training course conducted by Hunting with Slingsby Fireflies;

---

[59]The Provision of Engineer Officers in the Armed Forces: a Report by A F Frodsham CBE, December 1983, para 44
[60]Evidence, p 55, A4
[61]DCS, para 322
[62]Evidence, p 65, A4, (i)-(iii); *ibid*, p 73, A4

—the replacement of the Jet Provost by the propeller-driven Tucano;[63]

—the bringing together in one course at RAF Valley in Wales of the Hawk Advanced Flying Training and Tactical Weapons Unit courses.[64]

Other matters have been under consideration, including the role of Operational Conversion Units[65] and the adequacy of the Hawk's avionics as a training aircraft for the highly complex Eurofighter 2000 cockpit.[66]

25. FLF proposed a substantial acceleration of the trend towards civilianisation and towards tri-Service flying training. It also proposed, without any supporting argument, the closure of RAF Scampton and RAF Finningley. Scampton is the home of the Central Flying School: Finningley the location for training of a range of aircraft rear crew, including navigators, as well as of multi-engine pilots. FLF gave no indication of how these tasks would be met in future. Nor was it more forthcoming on multi-engine training: the text referred to looking at "a number of options", and the accompanying figure shows a large white box for Basic and Advanced Level multi engine training containing the words "In House/Collaborative/Civil Sector".[67] Air Vice Marshal Jenner, Assistant Chief of the Defence Staff — Costs Review, told us that, while civilianisation was one of a range of options, there had been no firm decision.[68] He also assured us that "the role of the Central Flying School will go on as now", but that the way in which its task will be disaggregated was still being studied.[69] In subsequent written evidence, MoD told us that the closure of Finningley arose from reduced requirements for rear crew. It is proposed to concentrate training aircraft types at nine individual locations, with basic airman and specialist aircrew training to be carried out on Bulldogs and Dominies at Cranwell, and navigator training at Cranwell, Linton-on-Ouse or Valley according to aircraft type. The CFS is in effect to be broken up, with the training of flying instructors carried out at Linton-on-Ouse or Cranwell according to aircraft type. Multi-engine pilot training is to transfer in the short term to another RAF station, not yet decided. There is no decision on the future location of the Red Arrows, nor various other units at the two stations. Consultative Documents on the closures have not yet been made available, despite the fact that both Scampton and Finningley are to close next year. **We are disturbed at the apparent absence of detailed planning before the decision to close RAF Scampton and RAF Finningley, which has left a number of unresolved issues.**

Command and Staff training

26. In July 1993, in response to our request, MoD provided a note on the outcome of a recent study into Command and Staff Training (CST), which had examined the costs and feasibility of collocating some or all of the single Service and joint Staff Colleges at a single site.[70] It was decided that, although there would be savings over a 20 year period, "the scale of the savings would be modest in relation to the initial capital investment required".[71] **It is noticeable that the study showed the set-up costs of a tri-Service collocation to be between £25 million and £35 million, to achieve 20 year savings of barely half that: and that cheaper and less ambitious collocations produced commensurately lower savings.** Some economies were however identified, producing 20 year savings of some £15.2 million for set up costs of £12.6 million: the move of the Junior Command and Staff Course from Warminster to Camberley and associated moves to Warminster from Netheravon and Bovington, increasing civilianisation of RAF Staff College instruction, and restructuring of

---

[63]See Report, HC 53 of Session 1980-81

[64]Qq 1377-8

[65]Qq 1387-9

[66]Q1384

[67]FLF, para 327 and Figure 8

[68]DCS Evidence, Q2681

[69]*ibid*, Q2682

[70]Evidence, pp 75-76

[71]*ibid*, para 2 and Annex

junior level courses. The RN already has junior and advanced staff training collocated at Greenwich — where the Joint Service Defence College is also based: **MoD told us that the scope for major savings in the future was limited.**

27. The proposal in FLF for a Joint Services Command and Staff College was explicitly not based on any financial savings involved. The Secretary of State's statement referred to "the joint Service nature of military operations", and in evidence to us he stressed that the decision had not been taken on purely cost grounds, although he told us "it will certainly make some saving".[72] His oral statement to the House seemed to be less firm on collocation of junior command and staff training on one and the same site:[73] nor is it wholly clear whether it is proposed that the Higher Command and Staff Course, which is to be expanded, will remain at Camberley regardless of the location of the new Joint College.[74]

28. **We extend a broad welcome to the concept of a Joint Services Staff College, while counselling some caution in assuming too readily that the excellence of the present institutions can be preserved in the sort of merger envisaged.** It is essential that officers attending the new course continue to receive a thorough grounding in, and continue to be instructed where appropriate by experienced officers of, their own Service. It is also imperative that all three Services come to regard command and staff courses at the College as a prerequisite for professional advancement, whatever the difficulties which seem to have prevented officers from some Services from availing themselves of such courses in the past.[75] We note the reference to a course length of a "minimum of 10 months", and hope that this will indeed allow of a longer course, and one that can lead to a recognised civilian qualification. We plan to visit Camberley and Greenwich in the near future, and will continue to monitor developments in the plans for a Joint Service Staff College.

29. FLF also identified certain shortcomings relating to the attendance of officers at the Royal College of Defence Studies (RCDS):

—selection of officers at an age where their experience and talents are needed elsewhere;

—removal of officers in mid-course for similar reasons;

—subsequent postings not making the most of training received;

—officers leaving the Service shortly after completing a course.[76]

As a result, a number of proposals are being urgently developed to rectify the situation, in time for the selection of students to be made in the first half of 1995 for the course beginning in January 1996. **It would seem that scrutiny of the RCDS has revealed what is in some respects a sorry state of affairs; we commend MoD for the sense of urgency in ensuring that the training at this level is both appropriate and properly used by the Services.**

Physical fitness

30. All Service personnel have to undergo tests and evaluation of their performance and skills at entry and regularly through their career, as a means of ensuring that the required levels of individual skill have been achieved in the training system, and equally importantly that they are being maintained. It would be reasonable to suppose that one common requirement would be a standard of physical fitness, easily measurable and relatively achievable. We note the recent reported comment of the Dutch Army's Chief of Staff, on introducing a fitness test, that "we ran the risk of becoming more and more like civil servants

---

[72]DCS Evidence, Qq 2593-7

[73]DCS Evidence, p26 and DCS, para 319

[74]FLF, para 321

[75]Evidence, p 54, A2

[76]DCS Evidence, p43, A11b; FLF, para 322

instead of soldiers".[77] While we see little risk of that happening in our Armed Forces, the new scenario of mobile and flexible forces means that physical fitness gains in importance not only for combat arms but also those in support who may be in equal danger and deployed in physically demanding circumstances. At the same time, an increasing number of Service jobs seem to involve sedentary skills, particularly computer skills. We also note recent reports that the physical robustness of Army recruits is below earlier standards, requiring remedial platoons in Army training regiments.

31. In the *Army*, all soldiers of all ranks and ages are required to take a basic fitness test involving a 1.5 mile run and walk in a squad for 15 minutes, followed by a 1.5 mile run in 10 minutes for those under 30, with a gradually rising increment for older personnel: those over 40 are permitted to take a similar test as individuals.[78] The current standards for women are lower, eg 12 minutes 50 seconds for female recruits for the 1.5 mile run rather than 10 minutes 30 seconds for male recruits; but the possibility of more stringent, and possibly common, standards for women is under examination.[79] There are no formal sanctions for failure, beyond having to retake the test, and the very distant possibility of discharge where limited personal fitness degrades an individual's usefulness to the Army without compensating benefits.[80] On 1 January 1994 *the RAF* introduced an annual fitness test for those under 50, geared to age, and consisting of an aerobic test and two muscular endurance tests, with a pedal cycle and hand-grip test. Those who fail — and very few have so far done so — are offered a remedial package, with the eventual sanction of dismissal.[81] Physical fitness tests were briefly introduced in the *Royal Navy* in 1976, but suspended on the death of two people taking the test, albeit with other contributory factors. A voluntary test was introduced in April 1993, based on running tests similar to those used by the Army for those under 40, and bicycle machine tests thereafter. Witnesses doubted the practicality of compulsory testing in view of the limited space on ships and constraints on time ashore.[82]

32. While we sympathise with the Royal Navy's difficulties, we note that physical fitness tests are widely used at RN entry training establishments, by the Royal Marines and at the Royal Navy School of Leadership and Management;[83] and we cannot believe that, in the course of a year, it should be unduly difficult for most RN personnel to find an opportunity to run 1½ miles. Our predecessors were told that the physical condition of submariners, whose physical conditions of service make regular exercise particularly difficult, was "regularly monitored", and recommended that further consideration be given to developing physical fitness programmes for submariners.[84] **While we have no reason to question the standard of physical fitness in the Services, we would expect those Services currently using voluntary arrangements gradually to evolve them into a more formal structure of testing.**

Skills

33. The most basic skill expected of all *Army* personnel is to be able to shoot accurately and effectively. All soldiers are required to take an annual personal weapons test (APWT). Figures provided by MoD show that, as might be expected, the infantry achieved a pass rate of 98 per cent in 1992/93. The rate for other combat arms was not so impressive: the Royal Artillery achieved 78 per cent and the Royal Engineers 77.4 per cent, rates exceeded by all other arms and Services.[85] While the average pass rate of 86 per cent is acceptable, **we are disturbed that, despite the perception that the introduction of the SA80 and its associated**

[77]*Armed Forces Journal International*, November 1993

[78]Evidence, pp 46-7, A7b. Those in combat arms are required to undertake a further combat fitness test: Q2176

[79]*ibid*; Qq 2194ff; SDE 93, para 754

[80]Qq 2176-8, 2191ff

[81]Qq 1352, 1366-8; Evidence, p 71, A1

[82]Evidence, p 55, A6; Qq 350ff

[83]*ibid*

[84]Sixth Report, HC 369 of Session 1990-91; for Reply, see Sixth Special Report, HC 674 of Session 1990-91, para 16

[85]Evidence, p 46, A6; Qq 2197-2201

**computerised training package should have made it easier to pass, a significant minority
of soldiers in teeth arms fail the annual shooting test.**

34. A further test and encouragement of shooting skills is provided by the Tickle Skill at
Arms Competition, based on APWT results on SA80 and the LSW. MoD told us that
infantry units were required to take part in the competition: but participation in recent years
has been decidedly patchy, with fewer than half of infantry battalions taking part in 1990/91
and 1991/92.[86] In 1992/93 26 infantry battalions took part, but only 11 other units. The
rate of participation is affected by the pressure of operational requirements; exemption from
the competition has to be sought from the Director of Infantry.[87] There may also be a
perception that the competition is unduly close to sporting shooting, and that it is the private
preserve of the Worcestershire and Sherwood Foresters (1 WFR), who win on a regular basis,
challenged mainly by Gurkha regiments. While we are much impressed by 1 WFR's
maintenance of their sharp-shooting traditions, it would be regrettable were shooting
competitions of this sort to be disregarded by the rest of the infantry, or by the rest of the
Army.

35. The apogee of Army shooting has long been the Regular Army skill-at-arms meeting
at Bisley. It was relatively manpower intensive, requiring around a company for two weeks
to administer the ranges.[88] Although the Director General Army Training told us that he
considered this type of competition to be entirely relevant,[89] a major review has now
concluded that it should be reduced to a one-day event, to be known as the Regular Army
Queen's Medal competition, with competitors selected from divisional and district meetings.
This format was adopted for the first time in 1994. The Minister's announcement referred
to new IGDT guidelines designed —

"to ensure a high standard of marksmanship throughout each Army unit, and that
resources are available to improve the less proficient as well as enhance the skills of those
who are already excellent shots".[90]

**We would welcome any step to improve shooting skills throughout the Army,
accompanied by measures designed to ensure that those soldiers who fail the APWT
receive the necessary instruction to improve their skills, and that as many infantry units
as possible take part in the relevant competitions. We note the importance correctly
attached in the past to UK performances in NATO skill contests with tanks, artillery,
guided weapons and so on: it is important that individual shooting skills be at least
equally encouraged.**

36. All recruits to *the RAF* undergo a seven week basic course at RAF Halton, which
includes Ground Defence Training (GDT), use of personal weapons and physical education.[91]
Under the Common Core Skills (CCS) concept introduced in the past few years, all RAF
personnel are required to renew their basic military skills annually, with more regular
refresher training for those required to carry arms.[92] Around 80 per cent pass the CCS test,
below the original target of 85 per cent, but rising. The CCS system has reduced the
requirement for attendance at annual training, and also the requirement for GDT instruction
from the RAF Regiment.[93]

37. The *Royal Navy* relies on its task book system for ensuring that individuals maintain
high levels of skills in such areas as firefighting and damage control and first aid and, for the

[86]Evidence, p 39, A2 and p 43, Annex C; Q2185
[87]Q2186
[88]Q2183
[89]Q2182-3
[90]HC Deb, 18 January 1994, col 507w
[91]Evidence, pp 71-2, A1. RAF Regiment gunners receive basic and specialist training in a single separate course: *ibid*
[92]Q1354
[93]Evidence, p 71, A1

minority required to bear arms, shooting skills.[94] This system has the advantage of putting much of the onus for annual performance measurement on individuals, and is intended to focus the attention of individuals on their specific role, but also on "the wider organisational environment".[95]

38. **It is of note that the Services already have in place a series of overlapping systems of individual assessment which could if required be used as a means of developing different pay arrangements: a matter currently under review. There are at present no obvious penalties for failure to pass a fitness or a weapons test, or complete a task book to schedule or pass the Common Core Skills test: nor any incentives to pass or excel. We await with interest the proposals to emerge from the Review of Service Career and Manpower Structures and Terms and Conditions of Service.[96]**

Adventurous training

39. Adventurous training is seen as an important part of military training in all three Services: as the Director General Army Training told us, it is regarded as

> "very much as a mainstream component of the overall training for war that a young soldier does, and in terms of junior leadership we think in many ways it is unequalled or unrivalled as a training medium for bringing on young people...".[97]

Because much of it is conducted at unit level, and in practice makes few additional calls on public funds, costs are not readily identifiable. Information placed in the Library in response to a Parliamentary Question shows that around £9.5 million is spent on operating costs, employing around 375 staff, divided equally between Service and civilian staff, and with a range of equipment for air, water and land.[98] There have been recent closures as a result of cuts, notably of the establishments in Norway and Germany; others such as the sailing centre at Kiel, have been reduced in scope.[99] The Minister of State for the Armed Forces recently announced that, as part of a wider review of Army-sponsored training, and separately from the DCS, MoD was studying "the scope for maximum efficiency and rationalisation of adventurous training", to report after the DCS.[100] **For relatively little expenditure, adventurous training offers the Services a chance to train young men and women in a potentially dangerous but unwarlike environment. As an essential part of armed forces training, we would view with concern any further cuts in the overall range and volume of opportunities available.**

IV COLLECTIVE TRAINING

Introduction

40. Collective training across all three Services is intended to maintain and enhance tactical operational capability at every level from a guncrew on a ship, an individual aircraft or a tank crew up to the largest operational formation levels. It embraces everything from classroom tuition to the engagement of thousands of people in a major exercise: and includes training for primary wartime roles and peacetime roles.

---

[94] Qq 342-4; Evidence, p 59, A5. For WRNS speed in task book competition, see Q384
[95] *ibid*
[96] SDE 94, para 514
[97] Q2184
[98] HC Deb, 26 May 1994, col 234*w*; Library Deposit, NS 10890
[99] Q2184; see Evidence, p 45, A5
[100] HC Deb, 21 June 1994, col 109*w*

Army

41. The Army has recently developed a collective training strategy, issued on 1 April 1993, which has been made available to us only in summary form.[101] It requires every unit to "train in the special to arm skills required for *their primary role* every year...":[102] no easy task given the strains imposed by the emergency tour commitment on, for example, Royal Armoured Corps and Royal Artillery units separated from their primary weapons. The requirement for all arms collective training is that all units should have had sufficient experience to be —

"sufficiently prepared to allow their deployment at the beginning of any warning period".[103]

It is not disputed that standards of all arms collective training have been eroded over recent years as a result of operational demands, amalgamations and movements, and the shortage of appropriate training grounds, notably with the termination of the use of Soltau Luneberg in Germany.[104] We have set out in earlier reports problems over using to the full the unrivalled battalion group facilities at BATUS. In 1992, we were told there had been a desperate shortage of infantry companies, and that 1993 prospects were poor.[105] We have now learned that in 1993 only five of the 12 required infantry companies were available, and armoured regiments exercised without infantry.[106] In July 1993 we were told that prospects for 1994 were better. We had hoped to be able to pursue a number of issues in the course of our visit to BATUS planned for September 1994, including the realism of the training in terms of equipments used and not used, and the extent to which other commitments mean that BATUS is in effect underused. **It is of course crucial that the facilities at BATUS should be fully used, and we will be pursuing this matter in future.**

42. There are also central directives as to:

—*the frequency of higher formation exercises*, emanating from SACEUR and from national authorities. Divisions are required to hold one CFX every four years and a CPX every year; Brigades one FX or CFX every three years, and one CPX every year. A Divisional field exercise is a thing of the past: even brigade-level exercises are rare.[107] The Director of Army Training was confident that the requirements would be met; other ways of formation training are being examined, including sending Brigade Commanders for "dry" training at BATUS, and the procurement of a Higher Formation Trainer.[108] The list provided to us by MoD, however, of FTXs and CFXs at battalion level and above for the years 1992-94 shows a substantial fall in such exercises in 1994, and in particular those on training grounds, despite the increased requirement following the return of forces from Germany. The ability of the three Armoured Brigades in Germany to hold realistic exercises, as well as the two Mechanised Brigades, 24 Airmobile Brigade and 5 Airborne Brigade in the UK, is open to question. For the recent 1 Brigade exercise First Crusade on Salisbury Plain, one of the three infantry battalions in the brigade was in Bosnia and another serving in Northern Ireland, with a squadron of the Brigade's armoured regiment similarly absent;[109]

—*the frequency with which weapon systems are fired*, constrained by the allocation of training ammunition, currently held at 74 per cent of previous levels, and being used up to the limit. We note the Director's confidence that the allocations are sufficient to allow realistic training. Although not avowedly used any longer as a financial regulator following

---

[101]Evidence, p 39, A3 and pp 43-4, Annex E

[102]*ibid*, para 6: italics added

[103]*ibid*, para 7

[104]eg Qq 2202-3

[105]Second Report, HC 306 of Session 1992-93, para 39

[106]Qq 2249-53

[107]Q2257

[108]Q2256

[109]HC Deb, 24 May 1994, col 108*w*; *ibid*, 14 June 1994, col 531*w*

a 1991 decision to this effect at the highest level, it is however evident that training ammunition is being restrained for financial rather than technical or military reasons;[110]

   —the maximum permitted tracked mileage, known in the Army as training datum levels, whereby a total annual mileage for each type of vehicle (eg 150,000 miles) is divided up among commands and passed down to each level, so that a particular vehicle in a unit has, say, 500 or 1,000 miles permitted in a year. The overall levels were cut several years ago to 85 per cent of the previous figure:[111] yet more alarming, other constraints — primarily the lack of training grounds — has meant that even these reduced levels have not been met.[112]

We conclude that a mixture of constraints means that the Army is denied the training opportunities it needs; that Army overstretch has degraded all arms collective training below the standards required; and that the Army's ability to field within the required time the full number of recently exercised battle groups and battalion groups has recently been compromised.

   43. The enhancements announced in connection with DCS included confirmation of a major programme of improvements to UK Army training areas, expenditure on which had been excluded from the transitional works expenditure agreed by the Treasury in PES 91. These include works at Otterburn to permit the use of MLRS and AS90, and major improvements on Salisbury Plain and Catterick to allow for more tracked armoured training. These proposals, which are not new, are to cost around £40 million over several years.[113] The announcement went on —

   "We also intend to increase our investment in the use of existing training facilities in Germany by units based there by some 50% compared with previous plans so enhancing levels of collective training, particularly at the battle group level".[114]

In oral evidence, AUS (Programmes) told us that around £4 million was being made available to buy range time at Bergen-Hohne, subject to competition for such time with other NATO countries.[115] In September 1992 we were given an estimated increase of around £3.2 million in the annual costs of the use of Bergen Hohne as a result of withdrawal from Soltau Luneberg.[116] The additional £4 million now made available, while wholly welcome, does not make up for the loss of Soltau Luneberg. Previous plans for the training year 1995/96 and beyond assumed the availability of "up to 6 weeks of battle group manoeuvre training between the 12 battle groups based in Germany": the additional funding —

   "should increase significantly the number of opportunities for battle group manoeuvre training, although the precise amount will depend on the availability of both units and range space".[117]

It remains essential for the maintenance of a properly exercised Armoured Division in Germany that it should have access to larger areas than Bergen Hohne for manoeuvre and live firing: and we look to the German Government to press forward with the possibility of the use of former WTO training areas in the Eastern Lander. **We will be seeking confirmation in the future that the promised increase in battle group training has in fact happened.**

   44. The Army is increasingly dependent on overseas exercises for realistic medium scale training, notably at BATUS in Canada — six exercises a year, three from UKLF and three

---

[110]Qq 2216-2229; Evidence, p 47, A8

[111]Q2205

[112]Qq 2206-7, 2210

[113]DCS Evidence, Q2699

[114]DCS Evidence, p28

[115]DCS Evidence, Qq 2699-2700

[116]SDE 92 Report, Evidence, p 65, Annex B

[117]DCS Evidence, p42, A9

from Germany: in Washington, USA — two exercises a year: and in Kenya — two or three exercises. Jungle training is held in Brunei and, from this year, Belize. There are prospects in other countries: for example, the Army holds annual company level exercises in Botswana, at the estimated additional cost of only around £65,000.[118] There were two company level and one battalion level exercises conducted in Jordan in 1993, as shown on the map in SDE 94: MoD referred in evidence to the "excellent opportunities" afforded by such training.[119] Foreign exercises cost around £10-15 million a year: although a number have political and diplomatic significance — for example, those in connection with the 5 Power Defence Agreement.[120] The FCO meets the cost of only one, the annual Red Stripe exercises with the Jamaican Defence Force.[121] The training provided cannot be provided in the UK: without it, the Army would quite simply be desperately short of training. **We would be dismayed were there to be any reduction in the resources devoted to overseas military training.**

Royal Navy

45. The RN's principal directives on regular training tasks is the Fleet Charge Document, which sets out in some detail the nature and frequency of a mass of training tasks and achievement targets intended to ensure that ships are maintained at a satisfactory standard of Operational Performance.[122] These include regular action stations and emergency drills, including machinery breakdown drills; replenishment at sea, with speed and safety criteria; and a range of over 50 damage control, firefighting and NBC drills, exercises and refresher courses. There are regular warfare drills, with infrequent live firings, and a range of objective fleet standards in all branches of naval warfare. In view of our comments last year in our Report on UK Peacekeeping and Intervention Forces that we suspected that naval gunfire support required some closer attention, we note with interest a recent change in emphasis towards greater first salvo accuracy.[123] A number of trophies are awarded annually for the best performance, including the splendidly named Good Luck Cup for small ships gunnery.

46. We have in the past reported our concern at the cancellation of some exercises for a mixture of financial and operational reasons, and in particular at the extent to which the fuel allocation was being used as a regulator.[124] It is difficult to discover whether planned exercises have been cancelled as a result of financial constraints, since plans are drawn up in the light of what will be feasible;[125] but we note that there has been a fall of almost 20 per cent in the fuel allocation between 1992/93 and 1994/95, excluding Adriatic operations, and that the fall in 1993/94 was not as bad "as originally planned".[126] **The evidence suggests that repeated cuts in the annual allocation of fuel to the Fleet may be constraining the number and nature of exercises in which RN ships can participate, which could lead in time to measurable deterioration of operational standards.**

---

[118]HC Deb, 25 May 1994, cols 218-9w

[119]Sixth Report, HC 68 of Session 1993-94, Evidence, p 121, A2

[120]Q2236

[121]Q2237; Evidence, p 48, A9

[122]Qq 368-372; Evidence, p 62, A13c. The document is classified.

[123]Fourth Report, HC 369 of Session 1992-93, paras 34-37

[124]HC 637 of Session 1992-93, para 17

[125]Qq 373ff

[126]Evidence, p 57, A8

RAF

47. The RAF conducts regular firings to ensure the safety and validity of its weapons, and to give aircrew the required levels of confidence. While they are pretty infrequent — strike attack aircrew will fire one Sidewinder in two tours, air defence aircrew will fire one Skyflash and one Sidewinder in each tour — the Assistant Chief of the Air Staff felt that, with around three sorties a week and a regular range slot, aircrew were receiving enough practice.[127] We have reported in our recent Report on low flying on the requirements as to hours flown annually at low level, and very low level: the RAF compares well in flying and simulator hours with NATO counterparts.[128] We have also been assured that fuel allocations are "adequate" and are geared to ensure that aircrew can indeed preserve the levels of currency laid down.[129] The enhancements associated with the DCS included an increase in monthly flying hours for all fast jet aircrew over the next three years from 18.5 to 20 hours a month, meaning a total increase of some 8,000 flying hours a year.[130] **Although this increase, together with the introduction into front-line squadrons of nine Harrier GR7s currently held in reserve, will increase the volume of low flying, including night low flying, in the UKLFS,[131] we welcome the increase in flying hours, and the concomitant increase in the proportion of combat-ready aircrew in each squadron who can be deployed on operations.**

Constraints

48. All Services are constrained in their training and exercising by funding: that is a fact of life. But all three Services are increasingly facing other constraints which if not solved or circumvented could produce a situation in which the requisite training could not be carried out. A major constraint is that of environmental protection, which affects in particular the Army, but is also a continuing pressure on the RAF's low flying training. Operational commitments mean that exercises have to be cancelled, and that personnel are unable to gain or retain currency or qualifications in roles other than those in which they are engaged: for example, pilots in operations over Yugoslavia, however valuable the experience, may miss out on training in other roles, as may armoured infantry battalions operating as UN peacekeepers, or artillery batteries as static prison guards. A particular problem has arisen for the Fleet Air Arm helicopter training programme through the frequent operational deployments, and occasional refits, of the recently procured helicopter training ship RFA ARGUS. In her absence, other RFAs have been used, when available, with inferior capacity: with the result of an 18 month backlog of incompletely trained helicopter pilots and additional burdens on those in front-line service.[132] There is also the simple problem of numbers: the smaller the Force, the fewer units will be available with or against whom to exercise. For example, the RN is increasingly constrained by the dearth of RN ships and submarines against whom to exercise. The cuts in the RN submarine fleet have made ASW training more difficult for ships, submarines and for ASW helicopters:[133] the withdrawal of Upholders means that other solutions are being sought, including a training submarine, and calling on increasingly stretched SSN time.[134] The procurement of expendable anti-submarine and gunnery targets for RN ships and aircraft deployed away from home waters is intended to make realistic training easier in times of operational commitment.[135] For the Army, it is difficult to fill all the available slots at BATUS, given operational commitments in Northern Ireland and elsewhere: and, as recorded above (para 42), difficult to field even a whole brigade for a major exercise.

---

[127] Q1358; Evidence, p 72, A3

[128] Q1372; Evidence, p 70, A1

[129] Q1359; Evidence, p 73, A3

[130] DCS Evidence, p28; Qq 2677-2680

[131] DCS Evidence, Q2692

[132] Qq 408, 412-3; Evidence, pp 57-8, A10

[133] Q409; Evidence, pp 57-8, A10

[134] Qq 399, 407

[135] DCS Evidence, p28

Simulators

49. The constraints on the availability of men, materials and physical space for realistic training and exercising has meant a growing dependence on simulators to complement and in some cases replace such activities. The use of simulators by the Armed Forces, and in particular by the RAF, was reported on as recently as November 1992 by the National Audit Office, and thereafter in October 1993 by the Committee of Public Accounts.[136] The NAO and PAC Reports concentrated on simulators in the *RAF*, noting that simulators in the past entered service too late, failed to meet users' needs, were not modified in line with parent equipment, and were of uncertain effectiveness: and that utilisation rates, where recorded, were low. MoD concluded that no reductions in the number of simulators was practicable, even apparently of the Hawk simulators. We have not therefore re-examined the matter in detail. We note however the proposals in Front Line First of anticipated savings in simulator procurement of £10 million a year from 1996/97 onwards by establishment of an in-house expert cell and other means, including increased mobility of equipments leading to reductions in the numbers required.[137]

50. The *Army* already operates many simulators for individual training on weapons systems, such as the SA80 rifle, and is now moving towards simulators for units, intended not to replace exercises but to bring units up to a certain pitch of ability beforehand so that full value can be obtained.[138] Tactical engagement simulators with direct fire laser systems are to be introduced this year, with the more ambitious — and very expensive — Direct Fire Weapon Effects Simulator simulating artillery fire due "in about 1997".[139] A fifth simulator is to be procured to enable concurrent simulated battle group training in the UK and Canada.[140]

51. We visited HMS DRYAD near Portsmouth, the *RN's* School of Maritime Operations as well as the RN's School of Submarine Training at Gosport, both of which have a significant number of the more complex simulators operated by the RN. At the former, where there are command team trainers based on the command system of most of the RN's principal warship types, we noted the absence of a Command Team simulator for the Type 23 frigate. The NAO had reported in December 1992 that —

"a Command Team simulator for the Type 23 frigate has consistently been deferred due to financial constraints, and is currently due in service some two years after the planned service date of the command system of the frigate itself..."[141]

Following our visit, we sought information on the timing of the delivery of the Type 23 simulators, known as Combined Tactical Trainer Stage 5 (CTT5).[142] MoD set out the stages of procurement which would have to be gone through, suggesting a September 1996 contract for development and production and a September 1998 In-Service Date. In the interim, there will be introductory skill trainers for individual operators: but the burden will fall on the ship's company undertaking a heavy on-the-job training load. MoD candidly accepts that "this may impact on overall operational effectiveness..." and also referred to CTT5 being needed "to avoid the disruptive effects of almost continuous on-the-job training caused by trickle drafting".[143] In response to our further questions, MoD told us that the original T23 Command System contract included the hardware and software necessary for a CTT, but that the initial requirement did not include funding for its development and production "as this was to be covered by the existing CACS 1 programme" — the programme which was acknowledged to have failed. Funding for feasibility studies for a CTT5 was

[136]HC 247 of Session 1992-93; HC 680 of Session 1992-93

[137]FLF, para 409 and DCS Report, Evidence, p45, A15b

[138]Q2257

[139]Q2258: for consequent industrial participation agreement with SAAB, see SDE 93 Report, Evidence, p 85, 28

[140]DCS Report, Evidence, p31

[141]HC 247 of Session 1992-93, para 5.7

[142]Evidence, p 53, A1

[143]*ibid*

approved in April 1991: meaning seven years before its currently planned ISD.[144] **While the failure of the initial CACS 1 T23 Command System caused some delay in the provision of a CACS 4 T23 Command System Trainer, it also seems that financial constraints and an underestimation of the urgency of provision of such a trainer have together led to a highly undesirable four year gap between the first Type 23 frigate entering service with a CACS 4 Command System and the associated Combined Tactical Trainer entering service at HMS DRYAD.** Although there is a sensible move towards more training being undertaken at sea, at all levels, linking ships to shore where appropriate, and so reducing the ashore training and refresher training requirement, we hope that MoD has rediscovered the need for the full training requirement to be addressed at the outset of a project and maintained throughout: and that, as reported, the Training Needs Analysis is well underway in relation to the New Common Generation Frigate.

Evaluation

52. Increased emphasis has been placed over recent years on development of objective systems of evaluation of the outcome of the cycle of training and exercising, so that Ministers and higher level commanders can assess the quality and preparedness of the Forces. In September 1992 we were told that a study into identifying more precise means of measuring defence output had found that —

> "operational analysis models could provide a methodology for the measurement of defence output, using operational performance indicators (PIs) for military capability, equipment capability and sustainability to assess operational effectiveness..."[145]

While these findings are considered, the Services are developing their own evaluation systems.

> —The *RN* operates CAPES, based on a range of PIs measuring manning, equipment availability and the levels of training achieved, now intended to cover all DD/FF by the end of 1994, and to be extended subsequently to the rest of the RN: "it is intended to set CAPES targets for incorporation in the Fleet Management Plan 1995".[146]

> —The *Army* introduced an OPEVAL system in April 1991, now extended from unit to formation:[147] it is also proposed to institute formal reports from the training organisations, including BATUS.

> —The *RAF* has a "range of indicators", but seems to rely more heavily than the other Services on the system of periodic tactical evaluations (TACEVALS) of units, carried out every 24 months. These act as —

> "a focus for a unit's training and exercise programme and is in itself a very useful measure of a unit's capability and readiness".[148]

It is by no means clear that all three Services have made equal progress along the road of evaluation of the outcome of training against pre-set objective standards, and with future targets incorporated in management plans. We were again told in October 1993, in relation to Army training, that —

> "The measurement of training outputs is being considered with the Defence Operational Analysis Centre".[149]

---

[144]Evidence, p 58, A11

[145]SDE 1992 Report, Evidence, p 14, A7

[146]*ibid*; Evidence, p 57, A7; Qq 361ff

[147]SDE 92 Report, Evidence, p 14, A7; Q2202

[148]Evidence, p 72, A2

[149]Evidence, p 48

It is really high time that all this study bore some fruit. **The desirable outcome is that future training tasks can be selected against an agreed and measured assessment of past performance and desired future achievement.**

CONCLUSION

53.   We have set out in this necessarily brief survey of aspects of military training a number of concerns, in particular over the constraints affecting all services. the relatively slow progress toward tri-Service arrangements and at the effect of some recent decisions. We have not specifically considered the training provided prior to, and in the course of, particular deployments, nor some specialised training: these are subjects which we will be considering in the near future. The Secretary of State told the House on 14 July 1994 -

"Equipment levels are themselves of little consequence unless they are backed up by intensive and highly developed training arrangements."

Training arrangements are currently in a state of major organisational change: once that is over, the time will in our view be ripe for a thorough review of the content of initial and continuation training of individuals and units, and for the introduction of rigorous and objective evaluation of the outcome. We also look forward to the time when resources will be available to provide fully sufficient training for all our armed services.

LIST OF ABBREVIATIONS

APWT	Annual Personal Weapons Test
ASW	Anti-submarine warfare
AWC	Air Warfare Centre
BATUS	British Army Training Unit Suffield
BFT	Basic Fitness Test
BRNC	Britannia Royal Naval College
CCS	Common Core Skills
CFX	Command Field Exercise
CinC	Commander in Chief
CPX	Command Port Exercise
CST	Command and Staff Training
CTT	Combined Tactical Trainer
DCS	Defence Costs Study
DD/FF	Destroyers and Frigates
DES	Department of Education and Science
DNST	Department of Nuclear Science and Technology
DTC	Defence Training Committee
FLF	Front Line First
FOST	Flag Officer Sea Training
FOTR	Flag Officer Training and Recruiting
FTX	Field Training Exercise
FX	Field Exercise
GCSE	General Certificate of Secondary Education
GDT	Ground Defence Training
HMS	Her Majesty's Ship
IGDT	Inspectorate General of Doctrine and Training
ISD	In-service date
LSW	Light Support Weapon
LTC	Long Term Costing
MoD	Ministry of Defence
MLRS	Multiple Launch Rocket System
NAO	National Audit Office
NATO	North Atlantic Treaty Organisation
NBC	Nuclear, Biological & Chemical
OST	Operational Sea Training
PI	Performance Indicator
RAC	Royal Armoured Corps
RAF	Royal Air Force
RCDS	Royal College of Defence Studies
RFA	Royal Fleet Auxiliary
RN	Royal Navy
RNAS	Royal Naval Air Station
RNEC	Royal Naval Engineering College
SACEUR	Supreme Allied Command Europe
SSK	Conventional-powered hunter-killer submarine
SSN	Nuclear-powered hunter-killer submarine
UK	United Kingdom
UKLF	United Kingdom Land Forces
UKLFS	United Kingdom Low Flying System
USA	United States of America

PROCEEDINGS OF THE COMMITTEE RELATING TO THE REPORT

THURSDAY 29 SEPTEMBER 1994

Members present:

Sir Nicholas Bonsor, in the Chair

Mr Frank Cook   Mr John McWilliam
Mr Bruce George   Mr Peter Viggers

The Committee deliberated.

Draft Report (Military Training), proposed by the Chairman, brought up and read.

Ordered, That the draft Report be read a second time, paragraph by paragraph.

Paragraphs 1 to 53 read and agreed to.

Resolved, That the Report be the Ninth Report of the Committee to the House.

Ordered, That the Chairman do make the Report to the House.

[Adjourned till Wednesday 19 October at Ten o'clock.

LIST OF WITNESSES

LIST OF WRITTEN EVIDENCE

MINUTES OF EVIDENCE

TAKEN BEFORE THE DEFENCE COMMITTEE

WEDNESDAY 7 JULY 1993

Members present:

Sir Nicholas Bonsor, in the Chair

Mr Winston Churchill	Sir Nicholas Fairbairn
Mr Michael Colvin	Mr John Home Robertson

Examination of Witnesses

MAJOR GENERAL R W M McAFEE, Director General Army Training, MR D DREHER, Command Secretary United Kingdom Land Forces, and COLONEL J N G STARMER-SMITH OBE, Colonel Army Training 2, Ministry of Defence, examined.

Chairman

2153. Good morning, gentlemen. Thank you very much for appearing before us. I think we shall have a fairly brief session today, aiming to end at about 12 o'clock. Can we look, first of all, at the soldier's initial training? Can you bring us up to date with the process of concentrating initial training at five centres, and identify the Phase 2 centres involved?

(Major General McAfee) Yes, I can indeed. As I am sure the Committee will know, we have rationalised our soldier individual training into five army training regiments. From memory that is at Glencourse, Bassingbourne, Lichfield, Pirbright and Winchester. The first of these Army training regiments opened on 1 April this year. I have some knowledge of them, having personally visited the Winchester site, which trains the Royal Armoured Corps, Adjutant General Corps, Intelligence Corps, Light Division and the Army Air Corps soldiers. From my own visit and anecdotal evidence, we believe that the product both of the recruit and the quality of training which he is receiving is at least as good if not better than that received previously under the old organisation.

2154. Can you tell us whether there is any change in what is being taught or is it really just an organisational adjustment?

(Major General McAfee) It is mainly an organisational change, Sir, and the raw recruits, irrespective of age or sex, undergo a ten week common military syllabus in all the areas which you would expect on an individual training organisation. Once that Phase 1 ten week common military syllabus is over, they then shortly afterwards progress to Phase 2 training, which is carried out at the Arms and Service depots, which prepares the soldier to join his first field unit or for operational deployment. I perhaps should say that accepting young servicemen and servicewomen into the Army at the age of sixteen and a half or slightly older, has of course created an element of concern in terms of acting in *locus parentis* in terms of generally avoiding any unfortunate incident or examples where we have not fulfilled our responsibilities and discharged our responsibilities in every respect to their parents and to the education system. So a study is running at the moment led by Brigadier Mountford, which will report in the summer, which will look at the ways in which we must very carefully handle these young men and women as they come into the Army and to make sure

that we make the transition from Phase 1 training at the Army training regiments to Phase 2 training at the Arms and Service centres as painless and as happy a process as possible because that is the time at which a young soldier may elect voluntarily to leave the Army. We want to assure that our wastage rates in that respect are kept as low as possible, and that the Army continues to attract a reputation as a good employer of young people.

2155. I am a little unclear as to what effect this has on the junior leader system. Has that had to be adjusted to take account of these changes?

(Major General McAfee) Yes, indeed, principally because of the lowering of the school leaving age the Army has decided to abandon the junior leader training system, and the last courses are now washing out of the training organisation. We will rely entirely upon the Army training regiments to produce the young soldier in the future.

2156. Does this not lose a centre of excellence, if I can put it that way?

(Major General McAfee) I think it would be true to say that the Field Army does have some regrets about losing the junior leader establishments, because there is no doubt that some of those young men went very quickly through the Army promotion system and became our future regimental sergeant majors or indeed in many cases that I know of became commissioned officers. However, the evidence, to be frank, is patchy, and although there are those who claim that generally they produce a very good product, I think the truth was that they produced a few very high calibre individuals, but within one or two years of joining the mainstream Army there was very little to differentiate between the junior leader product and the trained soldier from the normal training organisation.

2157. Has there been an increase in the proportion of soldiers under 17, for example, as a result of this?

(Major General McAfee) I do not have the figures to hand, Sir Nicholas, but I think, inevitably, because we are recruiting at an earlier age direct from schools, we anticipate an increase, and that is why the Mountford study has been commissioned to look at the implications of handling these young people.

2158. You have abandoned the plans, I think, you had for Bramcote and Harrogate?

(Major General McAfee) We have indeed, Sir.

[Chairman *Cont]*

2159. Why did you abandon those if there was a likely increase at that level?

(Major General McAfee) We felt that Army apprentice training and technical training could be perhaps more effectively, and equally well carried out at the Arms and Service centres, and that is how we intend to proceed in the future. It is part of the overall rationalisation plan.

2160. Was your recruitment for 1994 increased as a result of the February 1993 addback?

(Major General McAfee) The long term recruiting figures on which the Phase 1 training was predicated was a total of 119,000 Army, and we anticipate that if those numbers fluctuated as a result of the addback of the two battalions, if the numbers fluctuated for those reasons and also to make up for capping of infantry recruitment in previous years, then that steady state could go up by perhaps as much as 700 soldiers per annum. If that does in fact increase, and these figures are by no means certain, then we believe we may have difficulty in accommodating those extra numbers within the existing Phase 1 establishments, and we could in future be looking at building extra accommodation to undertake that additional training.

2161. So that I am quite clear, the 119,000 figure is post addback, and before that it was 160,000?

(Major General McAfee) Yes, indeed.

2162. You were recruiting to that level until then?

(Major General McAfee) That is right. The long term steady recruiting numbers were predicted as being 15,000 per annum. As I say, because of the addback of the two battalions and some additional recruiting for the infantry we anticipate that could rise to 15,700 per annum. If it does then I think we shall have to re-examine the numbers that we presently train at the Phase 1 establishments.

2163. Have you costed that exercise?

(Major General McAfee) Not yet, Sir, no.

2164. You are confident that you can accommodate that extra cost without adding costs elsewhere?

(Mr Dreher) Yes, we are resource constrained to some extent, but again if we face this problem we shall have to look at a number of the priorities to see how we can accommodate them.

2165. If you have additional costs for that accommodation you will have to make the saving to match it?

(Mr Dreher) It is quite likely.

2166. Will that come out of limited or ring-fenced budgets for accommodation, or out of the general training budget?

(Mr Dreher) It would come out of the general training budget.

2167. That manpower target goes through for how long? In other words, if I look forward to 1997, would you have the same target, or would you have a different figure in mind?

(Major General McAfee) The best evidence we have is that 15,700 would be the top figure that we are presently looking at.

2168. Will you be able to maintain the "capbadge integrity"?

(Major General McAfee) As I am sure you know, Sir, the Army Board is very much signed up to the principle of maintaining capbadge integrity at these Army training regiments. We are confident at present that we will be able to do that, except in the exceptional circumstances of backsqadding or similar events. However, I do not think we can absolutely guarantee to maintain the integrity of capbadge integrity were we to have to handle the additional 700, but equally I think it would be a temporary aberration and my personal observation from attending one or two of these Army training regiments is that the question of capbadge integrity is not a significant issue with the young recruit. The evidence was that they really had no strong view or no strong claim to regimental identify at that stage and were more concerned with bonding with the young people who joined on the same day, and deploying all the usual defensive mechanisms against their instructing staff rather than worrying about the colour of their beret or the size or shape of their capbadge. It does, of course, become a very significant issue in Phase 2 when they go on to their own Arms or Service centre.

2169. Can we look at officer training. I believe the first joint graduate/non-graduate course is just ending at Sandhurst. Has that thrown up any problems you are aware of?

(Major General McAfee) Yes. As you say, Sir, the first common commissioning course started in September last year, although recently the Commandant at Sandhurst did remind me there was nothing "common" about his establishment, and he would prefer to call it something else. Having said that, and I spoke to the Commandant some three weeks ago, they really had had no difficulty at all in absorbing the different strata of people that now go through this common commissioning course, whether they be straight from school or university or whatever. Perhaps it is too early to say, and I think I would prefer to wait until the evidence from that course has become rather more clear. Certainly nothing has been brought to my attention of a significant nature.

2170. Can you tell me what the percentage of graduates to school leavers was on that course?

(Major General McAfee) I think the figures is 48 per cent, but I may have to ask about that. I think it may be 48 per cent.

2171. 48 per cent graduates, more or less half?

(Major General McAfee) Yes, it is about half, from memory.

2172. Perhaps you could check on that figure. When I was last in Sandhurst, which was quite a few years ago now, it was stated to me that there was a very substantial difference in the needs of the level of training for graduates and school leavers. Specifically, a comment was made to me that the school leavers have no leadership experience.

(Major General McAfee) I think that is probably true. There is some largely anecdotal evidence from, for

[Chairman *Cont*]

example, the Regular Commissions Board to suggest that some of the young people who come to the Board today are less well prepared to handle some of the tasks which they are invited to perform at the RCB, related to some form of junior leadership. Much of this is anecdotal, but against it is an area we are looking at to make sure we are recruiting the sort of person we need in tomorrow's Army, and secondly that we are inviting them to undertake tests which are relevant to the training which they have already had in early life. We are changing or modifying our methods to try to identify potential leadership rather than actually recognising that there may be some deficiencies in that area. The Sandhurst course itself I believe has also recognised that there may have been some deficiencies in the instinctive leadership qualities of young people joining the Army over the last few years and has therefore developed a common commissioning course to be rather stronger on leadership than on the traditional rather low level and essentially infantry biased skills that they taught in the past, so there is an increasing emphasis on junior leadership rather than the nuts and bolts of the military skills which they can pick up later on.

2173. I think the specific point that I was really getting at was that the graduates at that stage, being more mature, were substantially more capable of taking on leadership responsibility without additional training and therefore if you are putting them with the school leavers on the same course in exactly the same way, either you are under-training one lot who need more or you are wasting your time for the ones who have already had it.
    (*Major General McAfee*) I think it is a very valid concern, sir, but I have to say that I have no evidence to indicate either way, but I am sure at the end of the present course we will have such evidence available.

2174. There are press reports that there was difficulty recruiting actually enough young potential officers for the Sandhurst course. Is there any truth in those rumours?
    (*Major General McAfee*) It is not strictly my field, sir, but I did happen to bump into the Director of Army Manning and Recruiting the other day and asked him this direct question out of personal interest, and he said to me that it simply was not true, that it was difficult to recruit sufficient numbers for particular courses in the year, the point being that when a young chap comes out of university he either wants to go into Sandhurst then or he wants to go round the world for a year and do something quite different and then join the Army later. Thus the Army tends to fall between two stools in seeking to attract graduates or indeed school leavers in the middle of the year, which is why they are neither fish nor fowl, so a certain amount of adjustment and persuasion has to go on to meet the totals for that particular course but officer recruiting figures are not generally, as I understand it, a problem.

2175. Something which perhaps ought to be looked at is the timing of courses to fit in more easily with that.
    (*Major General McAfee*) Yes, and I understand that is being done, sir.

Mr Colvin

2176. I wonder if the Director General could list the principal individual tests which soldiers have to pass. I have in mind things like shooting, fitness, NBC, and are there any developments that we ought to be aware of?
    (*Major General McAfee*) The individual tests which soldiers are required to carry out annually in the field Army within their own units in order to comply with what are called Army training directives are first of all the Army personal weapons test (that is a test of their skill with their own personal weapon); a nuclear, biological and chemical test, NBC test; a first aid test; a basic fitness test for the whole Army, and a combat fitness test for some of the teeth arms. Those are the essential training requirements which they must pass each year and the results of those tests are reflected up the chain of command to their respective formation headquarters for the medium on a form called "operation evaluation" or OPEVAL, and those returns are passed up the chain of command and collated at brigade and district level thereafter.

2177. What happens if a soldier fails?
    (*Major General McAfee*) If a soldier fails then he undergoes retraining——

2178. He or she.
    (*Major General McAfee*) He or she undergoes retraining and is required to pass the test at a second or third time round. There is, as far as I am aware, no finite limit on the number of occasions—I am talking now from personal experience; that is of command, not failure—on which he or she may sit these tests but there comes a point where the serviceman or servicewoman's usefulness to the Army is limited if he is unable to pass for example his basic fitness test and he then might be invited to resign, leave or be discharged, so there does come a limit.

2179. Does fitness include swimming?
    (*Major General McAfee*) No, it does not. It is not part of the basic fitness test. I might also add I should think in case I have misled you that the servicewomen's standards are different from those of the servicemen's, particularly in terms of the combat fitness test, but we are now looking again at the standards which we think women ought to be able to reach because there is a view now in the field Army, indeed held by the women themselves, that the standards are too low.

2180. As far as the APWT is concerned, what is the failure rate? Is there enough ammunition for re-shoots, and has the introduction of the SA80 actually improved the pass rate?
    (*Major General McAfee*) Yes, it has. Let me say first of all that presently OPEVAL returns indicate that the pass rate of the Army personal weapons test is around 80 per cent, and that fluctuates very slightly between generally 78 and 82 per cent, something like that, so it is a bit of a sinecure but it is not . . . indeed before I came here today I tried to establish whether or not individual standards had perceptibly gone up or down, and there is no clear evidence to suggest that they have indeed changed significantly one way or the other, but I would say that the introduction of the SA80 and its

[**Mr Colvin** *Cont*]

accompanying training package, a computerised device called a small arms trainer, has significantly raised the percentage of first time passes on the APWT. To be frank, it is an easier weapon to fire. It is less intimidating and it is more accurate than its predecessor, the self-loading rifle.

2181. We found that too. The Tickle Competition: you require all infantry units to take part in it, but in 1991/92 only 21 out of the 55 did. I wondered why that was. Is it a question of overstretch? Perhaps you could give us the figure for the number who took part in 1992/93.
(*Major General McAfee*) We will see if we have that specific figure for you, sir.

2182. Whilst the answer is winging its way to you, can you answer a question about the annual skill at arms meeting at Bisley because I understand that this involves considerable Army manpower on the ranges. Could you tell us how many soldiers are involved in that, whether there any plans to cut back and if so, have you discussed it with the National Rifle Association?
(*Major General McAfee*) I think it would be fair to say that the emphasis on individual marksmanship in the Army today is rather more important than it was during the cold war era where size and mass were everything, so there has been, with the increased commitment to peacekeeping operations, an increase in attention and interest in individual marksmanship for the peacekeeping soldier. The apogee I suppose of small arms shooting in the Army has always been the regular Army skill at arms meeting. That is where the apogee of individual shooting is brought together once a year and all Army units, all regular and territorial units, are encouraged to focus on RASAM and to try and raise overall the levels of shooting in their unit or battalion. It is my view that the type of competitions and ranges that are employed at the Pirbright complex are entirely relevant to the requirements of today. That is a fundamental requirement, that the competitions are strictly relevant in every respect, whether in terms of snap shooting or fitness or whatever. We do indeed continue to run the regular skill at arms meeting. It started indeed this week last Monday at the Pirbright/Bisley complex. In order to run that regular Army skill at arms meeting we do require a number of soldiers—I think from memory some 100 in all—for a period of two weeks to look after general administration of the ranges. In the past there have been inevitably pressures on the regular Army systems table which have led to the future of the regular Army skill at arms meeting being questioned and being examined. My own department is presently involved in an examination of the Army's future policy on competition shooting and what part RASAM should play in that system. In addition to that we are examining the numbers of soldiers involved to make sure first of all that it is cost effective and that we can afford to deploy these soldiers in view of additional pressures or other pressures in the regular Army systems table. I do not know what the answer will be yet. I am inclined to the view that the Army will wish to retain this apogee of individual marksmanship. What I do not know yet is how many soldiers will be involved in supporting it or where the competition will take place. At the moment the ranges

at the Pirbright/Bisley complex are the most appropriate for the competition, but there may be other options which we will also examine, and I would anticipate that report being produced certainly before the autumn.

2183. You will no doubt be discussing this with the NRA because I think I am right in saying as far as their Bisley meeting is concerned they provide all the teams for the butts and so on and do the administration, so there may well be a case for them also looking after the Army Bisley meeting, or are the Army involved also?
(*Major General McAfee*) The Army Rifle Association and the National Rifle Association are clearly very closely involved in our consultations and deliberations. The future of the National Rifle Association's own meeting at Bisley would clearly be placed I think in jeopardy or change were the Army either to cancel its RASAM or to move it elsewhere, and that certainly will be a factor in our deliberations.

2184. Can we switch to adventurous training now? There are rumours about cuts on the training being done at places like Norway and Kiel. Can you elucidate on that?
(*Major General McAfee*) Yes, I can, sir. First of all I should say that we regard adventurous training very much as a mainstream component of the overall training for war that a young soldier does, and in terms of junior leadership we think in many ways it is unequalled or unrivalled as a training medium for bringing on young people and again my own evidence of young British soldiers in the Gulf and the responsibility that they bore, and indeed in Northern Ireland, would underpin the value of adventurous training as a mainstream activity. It produces initiative, interdependence, and generally speaking we are very much in favour of it. Of course, with the drawdown in BAOR under options for change, adventurous training like everything else has come under scrutiny in order to ensure that we are producing the most cost effective product that we can. The result of that is to close the British Outward Bound centre in Norway which was a jolly good centre but, to be frank, expensive. Also we have closed down the Army mountain training centre at Silberhutte in the Harz Mountains in Germany and we have rationalised all our BAOR adventurous training if you like at one site at Sonthofen in Bavaria. In doing so, and in my previous job I again was involved in adventurous training in Bavaria, I think we have produced a better product, a better course and its more cost effective as well. I am not clear on the future of Kiel. I know it has been reduced in size and scope but it lies slightly outside my area and I am not absolutely *au fait* with what BAOR are doing in terms of rationalising off-shore sailing with adventurous training in Kiel.

2185. Can we get the answer on the Tickle Competition now?
(*Major General McAfee*) Indeed, sir. In 1991/92 twenty-one battalions took part out of a possible total of 55, 38 per cent. The total number of SA80 participants, if that interests you, was 2,640, of which 329 failed. That is a 13 per centure failure rate. In the light support weapon 6,503 soldiers took part with a rather dismal failure rate, and I cannot account for this, of 50 per cent.

[**Mr Colvin** *Cont*]

2186. Why did not more units actually take part, because the policy is for them all to take part?

(Major General McAfee) Certainly the Director of Infantry places a certain priority on the tickle test and encourages units, encourages infantry battalions, to take part, and in order to get exemption they must apply to him and have sufficient reason, and the reason I think would be operational commitments. I cannot be specific but I would think almost certainly that if I were to invite the Director of Infantry to explain the absence of a number of battalions it would be for operational reasons, either Operation Grapple or Hanwood or Northern Ireland or whatever.

2187. The figure for 1992/93 would be lower still and for 1993/94?

(Major General McAfee) It could be, but if you would like that information certainly we can produce it for you.

Mr Colvin: Thank you.

Chairman

2188. I have two or three questions before we move on to units. Could you tell us whether the fitness test is taken by all ranks, including generals?

(Major General McAfee) I took my basic fitness test in Battersea Park three weeks ago, Sir.

2189. You are looking fitter than some of my colleagues.

(Major General McAfee) It is indeed taken by all ranks irrespective of size, shape, or experience. The standards are marginally different for a chap of my age, and as one goes up the scale you are given some leeway. I think I am allowed some two minutes over my more junior colleagues.

(Mr Dreher) That does not apply to civil servants yet.

Mr Churchill

2190. On that point, Mr Chairman, what is the penalty in the event of failure?

(Major General McAfee) I think principally in my own case derision, and secondly, an invitation to repeat the performance, which is such a horrific prospect that one tries to pass first time round.

2191. What about those who have let themselves become so unfit that they are incapable of passing it? Is there any restraint on that?

(Major General McAfee) Yes, there is. A soldier or servicewoman is required to pass these tests. If they continually fail to pass them then they are invited to undergo a medical examination to make sure they are medically capable of undertaking it, and, if they happen to be overweight they are encouraged to undergo some form of remedial fitness training, and a reduction of weight, and then they are invited to take it again. As I intimated earlier, if the soldier continues to fail he places himself at risk of some sort of administrative action in terms of discharge from the Army or something of that nature.

2192. Does this happen?

(Major General McAfee) It does, Sir, yes indeed. I have to say again from personal experience, that of course you do get chaps who have perhaps become a little wide in the girth, and are physiologically unsuited to running. There are people like that. Equally, these chaps may be absolute paragons in the regiment in terms of being a super arms storeman, or as a bus driver or a tank driver, so there is a certain amount of leeway. Fitness is not the only measure, clearly, of individual performance in a soldier. A very unfit chap would have to have some other pretty damning features if he were to be thrown out of the Army simply on that basis.

2193. One does get the impression that the Army, including the senior echelons, is a whole lot fitter today than 20 or 30 years ago?

(Major General McAfee) That is undeniably true, Sir.

Chairman

2194. Except for those serving under Field Marshal Montgomery! I was slightly disturbed to hear you say that the tests women undergo are too low. In the event of combat their duty and fitness needs to be identical to men?

(Major General McAfee) Yes. It is slightly outside my field, but I should start by saying that of course at the moment women are not employed in the front line, as it were, in the Army, and, therefore, in general terms they are not required to carry out the full range of strenuous activities that a man would be expected to. Again, although it lies outside my field of confidence, I think, having spoken to the Director of the "Woman (Army)", last week, there is an acknowledgement that women are less strong in some areas, for example, in terms of upper-body fitness, and therefore, one simply cannot expect them, because of their inherent lack of strength in upper-body terms, and also because of their physical size, to lift the same weights that a man does. They simply cannot do it. On the other hand, aerobically women have shown that in terms of the basic fitness test which only involves running, most of them are just as capable of passing it as men. For all sorts of historical reasons the standards for BFT and CFT have been lower for women and, I think that the women find that rather insulting. The view in the Women's Army, amongst the women today is that their standards of fitness are high and the standards should therefore be raised. That is why there is a study being carried out at this moment to determine how and when those standards should go up. Certainly they will in the future.

2195. We saw women as signallers in Bosnia, and I have also seen them on sentry duty in Germany. I think there is a certain amount of concern that the fitness tests were not adequate, although they need not necessarily be identical.

(Major General McAfee) Yes, I think that is right, Sir. One would hope that the British Army in its traditional fashion can find some acceptable compromise that does not call for legislation in terms of the future employment of women in the Army. I do not think women particularly want to fire tank guns—that is the message that I get—but equally there are many other areas where they have proved to be immensely

[**Chairman** *Cont*]

useful, and I think those areas will expand in the future, but there are physical limitations.

Mr Churchill

2196. Whilst physical fitness is a very important element in all this, presumably toughness is as well. To what extent is close quarter unarmed combat, boxing and other sports such as judo, and karate part of the course, and is it not a field where women are at a particular disadvantage?

(Major General McAfee) I do not think I can answer that satisfactorily, Mr Chairman. I do not have detailed knowledge of the physical training syllabus of the Army training regiments, although again having visit Winchester recently the soldiers and servicewomen were undergoing physical training together, and I was unable to determine any difference in the syllabus between the men and the women, but I think boxing, for example, or milling, would only be carried out on a voluntary basis. I would not anticipate that the syllabus would have any difficulty in accommodating the different physical standards and problems that women might face. I am Commandant of the Army Physical Training Corps, and it is something which I will take an interest in in the future.

Chairman

2197. I look forward to coming down and seeing the ladies boxing! You said the pass rate in rifle shooting was 80 per cent.

(Major General McAfee) I did, yes. It is very difficult to be sure that standards have gone up or down because I think the pass rate figures this year were 78 per cent and 80 per cent last year, but there is no statistical data to show that they have fluctuated significantly one way or the other.

2198. That means that one soldier in five does not meet the proficiency level in shooting. Does that have consequences on how the soldier is going to be used?

(Major General McAfee) Yes.

2199. Obviously, he is not going to be a sniper. Would you put him in a situation where he is unlikely to participate in that kind of combat?

(Major General McAfee) I think generally one could say that standards in the infantry and those arms where the personal weapon is the primary weapon, are generally higher.

2200. Is that something you would have statistical records on?

(Major General McAfee) I am sure we would, Sir. We could certainly produce that. I think we would find very certainly a differing standard between those for whom the rifle is the principal weapon and those for whom the rifle is a personal weapon in terms of self-defence.

2201. Medical orderlies would be included in the statistics?

(Major General McAfee) Yes.

Chairman: Perhaps you would let us have that. Can we move on to training standards for units.

Mr Home Robertson

2202. I am sure I remember being taught in school that the female of any species was deadlier than the male! Moving on to training standards for units, I understand you have recently given the Committee some up to date information about training standards for units. Can you tell us what steps are taken to ensure that all units reach those training standards set out in the document you have given us?

(Major General McAfee) Certainly. Perhaps I should say first of all that there is a perception that standards of all arms collective training have suffered some element of erosion over the last year or so. I should also add that we expected that would happen, and it did not come as a surprise. Clearly, there have been additional demands on the emergency tour plot, principally operation Grapple in the former Yugoslavia. We have suffered a great deal of turbulence arising from the amalgamations and disbandments under Options for Change, so for example, the first and the third divisions in Germany closed last year, and the third United Kingdom division only became operational on 31 May this year. We have lost, or are in the process of losing our major training area in Soltau in Germany. That is Soltau Luneberg. There are certain shortfalls in existing Army field training centres, that is the major training areas in the United Kingdom. Finally, of course, we have had to pay growing attention to the environmental lobbies against the increased use of Army training land. I spoke of perceptions because there is always some difficulty in establishing just exactly where our collective training standards are, because military judgment has in the past played a rather large and inevitably subjective part. If I may go back slightly and say that in 1991 we set up a headquarters of the Inspector General of Doctrine and Training, whose purpose it was to draw together the two strands of doctrine and training to produce, if you like, a common philosophy, a common language, and a unity of effort for Army doctrine and training, and arising from that establishment were a number of tools which we intend to use for setting and evaluating standards. The first of those is a thing called the Army Collective Training Strategy paper, which was issued on 1 April this year, and something called, rather wordily, a Compendium of Collective Training Tasks, which is no more than a menu or a handbook from which formation commanders may draw appropriate training objectives for their units in that training year, depending on the standard that those particular units have reached. I mentioned before the operational evaluation return. Those reflect collective training standards during the year, and will tell us whether or not those units have reached the standards which have been set for them. In addition to that we have introduced a return called a Formation Evaluation Report which will serve the same function for brigade and divisional level. We are also moving towards introducing formal reports from the brigade and battle group training organisations, and also units passing through the British Army training unit in Suffield. I have to say, that these initiatives have not been in place long enough, or over a sufficiently representative period, to have any unequivocal answer for the Committee this morning, in other words, had the formations and units reached the critical level of military capability, which is the level they must be at

[Mr Home Robertson Cont]

at the start of transition to war. But I think I can say, Sir, that reports from both commands, BAOR and United Kingdom Land Forces, indicate that there has been an erosion of collective training standards, but not to the point at which it gives us great cause for concern at present. We have introduced a number of initiatives this year, and indeed in the future, which I hope will overcome some of these training deficiencies. I should say, of course, that the situation is worse in BAOR for the three armoured brigades and their heavy armoured fighting vehicles. It is less of a problem in the United Kingdom, for the lighter and less environmentally unfriendly intervention formations of the third United Kingdom division.

2203. It will come as no surprise to this Committee to hear that overstretched turbulence and other factors are having a harmful effect on the standards of training. I take the point that you are analysing this situation. It is disturbing to hear that significant numbers of units are falling below the standards set by the criteria you have been referring to. Are you analysing the detailed problems, or could you let us know privately the nature of the units which are specifically below the standards of training you would like to expect?
(Major General McAfee) On that point I should just say, if I may, that we have no evidence at the moment that collective training standards have dipped below the critical level that we require but I think there is a general acceptance across the theatres that there has been some erosion of standards. We do not have the data yet but I have the anecdotal evidence of for example the Commander of the British Army Training Unit at Suffield who feels, in conversation with me, that collective training standards have deteriorated somewhat, as we expected they would.

Chairman

2204. It must follow, must it now, just as a matter of logic that if you have an artillery regiment which has not fired a gun for two years, understandably the training is likely to be inadequate?
(Major General McAfee) Indeed, sir, although in referring to that unit I think you will probably find that was heavy regiment in Dortmund and I think I can reassure you slightly in saying that of course while the regiment did not fire in its entirety for operational reasons (that is, for reasons of operational commitment), of course the batteries and the troops themselves did fire, and I am sure that one could find individual evidence like that if one looked hard enough.

Mr Home Robertson

2205. Yes, but you are changing the criteria in some areas, are you not? Just to refer specifically to track training datum levels which you have given us details about, what is the significance of allowing only 85 per cent of the base line figure and now making that lower figure the base line?
(Major General McAfee) If I may, I will turn to Colonel Starmer-Smith who will elaborate on TDLs.
(Colonel Starmer-Smith) Across the board, sir, in fact training datum levels for track mileage have been set at some 85 per cent as you say. We have not actually exceeded those figures with any equipments except for

MLRS, so it is not a limitation at present on the amount of training that we do. Greater limitations are in fact the availability of the training areas on which that training can be done.

2206. What do you mean when you say you have not exceeded that level? Has the standard been reached or has it not been reached?
(Colonel Starmer-Smith) That is a figure of the amount of mileage which we may use in terms of track level. Each vehicle is given a mileage per year which it may cover. I have the figures. Across the board we have not used that mileage.

2207. You are below it?
(Colonel Starmer-Smith) We are below it.

2208. Are you suggesting that is a good thing? How can you achieve the level of training that you require if you are not meeting the target figure, and in fact have you not reduced the target figure to 85 per cent of what it was before?
(Colonel Starmer-Smith) It has not greatly reduced it. The figures are set on the availability of the equipment, the availability of the manpower and all those factors.

2209. So you are satisfied that you are not watering down the standards for track training too far?
(Colonel Starmer-Smith) What I am saying is that the limitations on the track mileage are not the cause of us not reaching those standards. There are other factors in terms of the availability of troops and so on.

2210. All right; never mind why it has happened. It has happened. We are now in a position where track units are getting substantially less training.
(Colonel Starmer-Smith) They are getting less training and the critical item of that lesser training is not the availability of the track mileage. It is the availability of either the troops who take part, the training areas, particularly in Germany, or other commitments.
(Major General McAfee) But you are right, sir, in inferring I think that from an Army standpoint we would like to see formations and commands saying to us: "We have reached these TDLs and they are not enough. We want to do more." We would be only satisfied in terms of collective training across the Army if they were reaching those TDLS that have been set for them and in some cases perhaps exceeding them or asking for authority to do so.

2211. I take it from that that the failure to achieve those targets must be degrading the capability of the units concerned.
(Major General McAfee) To some as yet unidentified extent but as I say we are looking at producing the tools to measure what those levels will be in the future and whether people are reaching them or not.

2212. Is that 85 per cent figure going to become the base line?
(Major General McAfee) It is the base line.

2213. Or do you want to take it back up to 100 per cent?

[Mr Home Robertson *Cont]*

(Major General McAfee) If the resources were available and we were able to train to that level, then of course we would like to have it at 100 per cent, but it is not in itself at the moment the major limiting factor.

2214. The same point in relation to training for units with non-armoured vehicles, B vehicles. Is it the same story?
(Major General McAfee) Yes.

2215. Do you want to elaborate?
(Major General McAfee) I think just that there are many other pressures that I have explained earlier and this is not the only limiting factor. It is simply one of the many.

2216. Take an example: are there levels defining how often a gun should be fired and how far the outcome should be monitored?
(Colonel Starmer-Smith) The answer on that, sir, is yes. We have limitations on ammunition. We have an agreed datum level of 100 per cent for training ammunition across the board for all weapons systems, be it guns, tanks, small arms and so on. At present our resource limitations reduce us to 74 per cent across the board in terms of the allocation of ammunition. Again of course, if resources were available we would like to go to 100 per cent, and that is an area of course where we do tend to get somewhere near the 74 per cent level of expenditure, but in a pure world if there were more resources available, yes, of course we would like to go to 100 per cent.

2217. Are there artillery pieces which are just not being fired year after year?
(Colonel Starmer-Smith) No, there are not. Every weapon system that I am aware of has been fired.

2218. Within the past how long?
(Colonel Starmer-Smith) Certainly within the past year. I am aware of every weapon system having been fired, including MLRS.

Chairman

2219. If an artillery regiment is in Northern Ireland doing infantry work, then are you saying——
(Colonel Starmer-Smith) Exactly. They are out of action for a period of six months during that time.

2220. It is more than that, come to think about it.
(Colonel Starmer-Smith) They have got the training time beforehand and the time afterwards. We do allow a carry forward or a carry-over of ammunition. Each regiment gets through an allocation of ammunition per year. We allow a carry forward of that ammunition so they can take it forward to the next year. We do have some flexibility in the system to allow for Northern Ireland or other emergency tours.

2221. But you would not transfer that allocation to another unit?
(Colonel Starmer-Smith) We do not normally transfer it to another unit, no. It is destined for a unit and they keep it as far as possible.

2222. Do they use it?
(Colonel Starmer-Smith) They do, yes, as far as I am

aware. I happen to be a gunner and I know that in my experience we have done just that. You certainly do not hand it over to another regiment who fire it.

Mr Home Robertson

2223. What are the principal constraints on the amount of training that units can do apart from limits on mileage?
(Major General McAfee) It might be for example the availability of Army training land and in particular of artillery and armoured corps ranges. There are pressures on these, particularly in Germany where we share many of the facilities with our allies, and as I mentioned earlier, there are growing constraints, both environmental and others, which limit the amount of time that we are allowed to use some of these training facilities. We are making significant efforts principally in the area of simulation to overcome some of these difficulties.

2224. Those are if you like external constraints. How about the internally generated constraints like ammunition and fuel? Has the supply side of blank ammunition problem been solved?
(Mr Dreher) I would say the answer is yes. There has been a shortfall of training ammunition in the past, we have conceded. The information now is that we have an adequate supply of training ammunition, and indeed apparently we are going to a new contractual process of five year contracts which will, we hope, guarantee supply, so at the moment there is no problem with training ammunition.

2225. So the allocation to units of live and blank ammunition is not being used as a regulator?
(Mr Dreher) Not at the moment.

2226. Not at the moment. Has it been in the past?
(Mr Dreher) Obviously it has, yes.

2227. And it could be in the future?
(Mr Dreher) Well, again it depends on the resource situation in the future.

2228. How about fuel then? Is the supply of fuel for training used as a regulator?
(Mr Dreher) I would say again probably not, but in resource terms because we are resource constrained we have to look at the totality of resources available for our training activity and take a view. It may well have been in the past from time to time that these have acted as constraint.

2229. Do units have fuel allocations or do they just draw what they need?
(Mr Dreher) I do not know.
(Colonel Starmer-Smith) Each unit is given a budget in terms of resources of which fuel is one and therefore you can make a balance between doing a particular activity in terms of where you do it, how far you need to go to get there, what type of training you do when there. It is within the judgment of that commander of that unit or that formation, this balancing of assets you have and the budget you may have. If I could just mention about the ammunition side, I would say that ammunition was used as a regulator but a decision was

[**Mr Home Robertson** Cont]

made at the highest level in the Ministry of Defence about two years ago that for the future, as far as ever possible, ammunition would no longer be used as a regulator to help balance the budget. Therefore we have very good fixed levels of ammunition for training.

2230. But at the end of the day the unit commander has got an overall budget and he has got to decide where to spend his money, whether on ammunition or on anything else.

(*Colonel Starmer-Smith*) Ammunition is a set figure; he is given that. He has some flexibility with fuel because it can be something that can be balanced against in terms of rations. It means if he is stationed in Plymouth he can go and use Okehampton ranges as opposed to Salisbury Plain, and the same in Germany, so he has that flexibility within the training system to choose where he wants to do his exercise, the type of exercise he wants to do—does he want a defence exercise, on which he can impose limits on fuel, to an advance to contact on which he uses a lot of fuel, so he has that balance within his training to give him some flexibility.

2231. Finally, have there been any instances when a commander has had to decide not to take up an opportunity for training on a range or wherever because he has run out of his fuel budget?

(*Major General McAfee*) I have never been aware of that happening in my service in terms of fuel alone.

2232. Or any other?

(*Major General McAfee*) You mentioned blank ammunition. Clearly the quality of your training can be enhanced or indeed diminished according to the amount of training ammunition or pyrotechnics that one has.

2233. Better than shouting "Bang!", you mean?

(*Major General McAfee*) Absolutely, and I have never come across any soldier who would not gratefully have at least 100 per cent more than you ever give him in those terms. Generally speaking I think on blank ammunition and pyrotechnics we get about enough to train realistically. We would always like more blank ammunition. It just adds to the interest and quality of training.

Chairman

2234. There are still sufficient thunder flashes about to put down the chimneys where the generals are staying?

(*Major General McAfee*) It is no longer allowed, sir.

Sir Nicholas Fairbairn

2235. Can I ask you how, where and by whom the minimum frequency for exercises at unit, brigade level and above are decided and how the priorities are fixed?

(*Major General McAfee*) Indeed, sir. Perhaps I could start by saying that within Allied Command Europe the Supreme Allied Commander, through the medium of a study called the Right Mix Study, has determined guidelines for formation training activity levels and in addition, within Allied Command Europe the new ACE Rapid Reaction Corps, in concert with SHAPE, is developing the exercise frequency for itself and ARRC assigned units. I could go on to say that within these Right Mix guidelines, to give you some specifics, a division is required to carry out one divisional level command field exercise, which is a combination of command post exercise and a field exercise on the ground, every four years, one CFX every four years and a command post exercise every year. Brigades are required to carry out one exercise a year including one FTX or CFX every three years, and these are national guidelines. These are guidelines issued if you like for national consumption, but in addition to that exercise frequency we are also of course required to carry out exercises within the NATO framework on a multi-national basis, so if you like there are two requirements—the multi-national requirement and then those required of SACEUR but within the national framework to meet training levels. I think I can confidently say that the British Army has always met these datum levels and anticipates being able to do so in the future.

2236. With regard to these exercises overseas, what are the principal costs? If we take something like air transport, I take it that is a principal cost. Does the Army repay the Air Force or does it go out to tender?

(*Mr Dreher*) No, I think the answer at the moment is that transport provided to the Army by the Royal Air Force is not paid for by the Army. It may be that in the future this may be a cost to the Army. My information is that at the moment it is not.

(*Colonel Starmer-Smith*) That is correct, yes. There have been two occasions in the past two years when we have had to use charter aircraft purely because the RAF transport support was not available. Those are exceptions. It is not the normal rule. We do not pay for the use of RAF aircraft. As regards the reasons for overseas exercises, they are obviously looking at areas and types of training facilities we cannot find in the United Kingdom: jungle, desert, arctic warfare. The requirements to try to export training if we can is to give variety, to give us facilities which are not available in the United Kingdom, and BATUS is the obvious one, to meet commitments or requests in terms of political aims which I would say particularly at the moment, for example, is the requirement to exercise as best we can in the Middle East. There is only one exercise a year which is not funded by the Ministry of Defence which is in the Caribbean. Those are the sort of things we look for, and of course there are the interests of soldiers, the good training we do in places like Kenya, Botswana, the variety that we get, and of course our requirement to take part in exercises with other nations where we have treaty commitments. I can think particularly of the five power defence agreement in the Far East, for example, where we do exercise each year either on a command post exercise basis or on an FTX basis. There is a variety of reasons why we exercise overseas.

(*Mr Dreher*) This gives us tremendous value for money. The amount of money we spend on the United Kingdom budget on these exercises as against the level of the budget is very small indeed. It is perhaps in the region of £10 million to £15 million, against a budget of over £2 billion. So it is tremendous value for money.

Chairman

2237. Who does pay for the Caribbean exercise?
(*Colonel Starmer-Smith*) The Foreign Office pays for that one. It is exercise Red Stripe in Jamaica.

Mr Colvin

2238. How do we train, as we are going to have to now, for more rapid deployment, bearing in mind we do not have any heavy lift air transport? What do we do when there must be rapid reaction and we have to deploy quickly? Are there any training schemes arranged for that contingency because at the moment we do not have the aircraft available, so how do we train to deploy quickly should the need arise, which is highly likely?
(*Major General McAfee*) Clearly, nationally we rely either on the RAF or the Air Transport Fleet.

2239. We cannot get an MLRS into a Hercules, not even with a shoe horn, and the Warrior will not go in either.
(*Major General McAfee*) Indeed not. Then indeed as with the arrangements for the Gulf, one would either take up shipping from trade, or if one was involved in a coalition operation hope that one of our allies, either the Russians or the Americans, would also be involved as they are the only nations, of which I am aware, that have a strategic airlift of that capacity and capability.
Mr Colvin: They are the only two we are aware of as well.
Mr Robertson: You refer to the Russians as our allies. I like that.

Chairman

2240. I hope they remain so.
(*Major General McAfee*) Coalition partners perhaps is better.

2241. Can I come back to the central theme? What are the principal costs? We have mentioned air transport. What are the other principal costs of overseas training?
(*Major General McAfee*) As Mr Dreher, the Command Secretary has indicated, the overseas training exercise costs vary from £10 million to £15 million per annum, which I understand is quite a small proportion of the overall training budget. Although that can rise to around £30 million if we are involved in a major purple field training exercise. I would say on average £10 million to £15 million, rising to £30 million for a major exercise on a tri-service basis.
(*Colonel Starmer-Smith*) I think it depends a lot, Sir, where we go in terms of what it costs, depending on what facilities are available in countries. For example, we do a lot of small company exercises in Cyprus. Because the facilities are available in Cyprus that is a relatively cheap exercise. If we go to somewhere like Botswana where we have to take a large amount of facilities with us then it becomes more expensive.
(*Major General McAfee*) I can be specific and tell you that for example exercise Pond Jump West, which the infantry undertake in Canada costs £25 per day per man. A similar exercise Lion's Sun in Cyprus costs £1 per day per man.

2242. You have those figures for virtually every exercise, do you?

(*Major General McAfee*) Yes, I do, Sir.

2243. On the question of prospects for future exercises, you mentioned there was one place in the Middle East where you can go. Are there prospects of exercises in countries such as Egypt, Morocco or Jordan?
(*Major General McAfee*) We are examining the possibility of extending or exporting some of our training elsewhere, and certainly we have been looking at the possibility of an MOU both with Egypt and Morocco, but we have made no significant decisions or headway as yet.

2244. Do you get full co-operation from the Foreign Office in those exercises?
(*Major General McAfee*) Yes, we do. We have sent people to those countries and they have been supported by the embassies, and had discussions with those countries. We are looking at producing a memorandum of understanding, which is a prerequisite for exercises in those countries. There are some technical problems, and I think that is what is holding us up, but we have good support from the Foreign Office.

2245. On the question of Brunei and Belize, it would seem that we have jungle training facilities in those two places. I think I am right in saying that it costs £2 million to train in Brunei. Have you any comparable figure for what it might cost to use Belize?
(*Colonel Starmer-Smith*) No, because at the moment we have only been sending companies to Belize to exercise in the last year, but as part of the rundown of Belize and the restructuring of Belize that will happen, then we are likely to set up a training base perhaps at collective level. We have no costs at the moment. It is still under consideration.

2246. I have been told that the savings for withdrawing our standing forces in Belize is £9 million, and I wonder how that figure is reached if nobody can tell us what the costs are of the training exercise that will replace them?
(*Major General McAfee*) I am afraid I do not have those figures, Sir.
(*Colonel Starmer-Smith*) I understand that £2.5 million a year is the plan for exercises in Belize.

2247. Are you satisfied there is the need for jungle training in Belize and Brunei?
(*Major General McAfee*) At the moment we undertake individual training in Brunei, where the topography is rather more suited to that style of training, and collective training in Belize. We have an agreement with Brunei at the moment which remains in force until 1998. Again my own Department is involved in looking at the Army's future requirements for jungle training and I would anticipate having a decision on where, how and when by the end of the year.

Mr Churchill

2248. What constitutes a full battle group?
(*Major General McAfee*) Broadly, Sir, two squadrons of armour, two companies of infantry, a battery of Royal Artillery and a squadron of Royal Engineers, plus other supporting arms. That is the normal package for a Medicine Man exercise.

[Mr Churchill *Cont]*

2249. From information you gave us late last year it is clear that the six BATUS exercises in 1992 were generally short of infantry, meaning that some armoured regiments had to act as infantry, or that only one company was available. We gather that 1993 has been worse, with the Cheshires and 1st Prince of Wales Own being in Bosnia, so that only five rather than 12 companies are to be provided for the six exercises including a company from an airmobile battalion out there now. Will you be able to field the companies you had hoped for to numbers 4 and 5 or will Bosnian commitments intervene?

(Major General McAfee) On present planning, sir, there will be a shortfall of infantry companies available at BATUS this year and indeed on the first two Medicine Man exercises we have no infantry at all. We sent four squadrons of armour on the first and four squadrons of armour on the second. Thereafter for the remaining four exercises we will distribute equally five companies of infantry which, as you indicate, is well short of the normal allocation of 12. We anticipate, providing there are no additional operational commitments, that we will come back up to the ideal of 12 companies next year, and I might just add that although certainly in terms of pure all-arms training there has been an erosion of standards, nevertheless BATUS offers in the round an extraordinarily good training facility for almost any form of training, but yes, certainly our armoured training has been reduced somewhat.

2250. I think there is no question of the enormous value of the facilities available and I think the question—and it is one which concerns this Committee very much—is whether we are in fact making proper use of those facilities that are available to us. You mentioned that four squadrons of armour had been sent. Does this mean that in those cases two of the squadrons are having to act as infantry, or how do you work that?

(Major General McAfee) I should say that the Commander of BATUS has had to adapt his normal training cycle to accommodate both the equipment and the organisation which he has had for any particular Medicine Man, so in some cases you might find armoured soldiers acting as infantry, but in other cases it might be that the——

2251. In Warriors?

(Major General McAfee) In 430 series vehicles. I should say in general terms it would be not too difficult for an armoured corps soldier to convert quickly on to Warrior but the case would not be the same in the reverse, not that that case exists, but there has been a certain amount of adaptability of mind necessary to training at BATUS this year.

2252. Just to clarify the situation, given your definition of what constitutes a full battle group, which you gave us a moment ago, how many of the six training exercises at BATUS in 1992 were up to full battle group strength and how many in the current year?

(Major General McAfee) If you would give me a moment, sir, I think I could have those figures to hand.

Chairman

2253. I think we actually have those figures on our records in the office.

(Colonel Starmer-Smith) If I may add, Chairman, the first two Medicine Men this year, they just used armour. They did not convert to infantry. They took maximum advantage of the equipment that is pre-based there and I understand from BAOR who were responsible for the exercises that they had extremely good live firing and other exercises albeit without infantry.

Mr Churchill

2254. What does the 1994 plot look like?

(Major General McAfee) The 1994 plot is rather better, sir. We anticipate having the normal battle group complement available at BATUS next year, providing there are no additions to the emergency tour plot.

2255. For all six exercises?

(Major General McAfee) Yes, sir.

2256. Is it not a matter of concern to you that we now have an Army where there are battalion commanders who have never trained with their full battalion and brigadiers who have never trained with their brigades?

(Major General McAfee) It does, sir. I think we have come to realise that it will no longer be possible to train battle group and brigade, and indeed divisional, commanders using the traditional methods that we have employed in the past, and that is why we are looking at new ways of training. If I can give you a couple of examples, once we are out of this period of, shall we say, restraint we are seeking to send brigade commanders out to BATUS to train their own battle groups on dry training and so Commander BATUS will look after live firing aspects, and the brigade commander will train his battle group and his own headquarters on dry training. We are also extending the scope of the brigade and battle group trainers to train brigade commanders and we are looking at new methods of simulation, such as a system called the Higher Formation Trainer, which will come into service next year and can be used very effectively—I have seen some of the prototype models—to train formation commanders, so we will be doing things differently; of that there is no doubt. The important thing of course is to strike that balance between field training, where the commander is faced with the physical consequences of his actions, and simulation where the same *frisson* of fear or excitement or success cannot be simulated quite so successfully. I am afraid for the reasons I gave earlier, we can no longer expect to deploy in the foreseeable future on major formation exercises over open ground. The climate in central region and, of course, in the United Kingdom will simply not allow that to happen in the future.

Chairman

2257. I think we should move on to simulation given our time constraints and the fact that soon we will not have a quorum. As you said that is going to change the whole way in which training will be undertaken. It is going to be very expensive upfront. Are you funded for that additional capital cost adequately?

(Major General McAfee) Yes. In a sense we have

[**Chairman** Cont]

always worked on the principle of training paying for training, so, for example, if we want some new gun simulator then we may have to take a reduction in the amount of ammunition that we would normally live fire. That is entirely appropriate because we have come to realise that simulation cannot do the job on its own, but what it can do is to bring a soldier or unit up to a certain standard of training in barracks before he deploys in the field. So when he goes out in the field he makes more effective use of the facilities which he is given, and the mistakes are made in barracks on simulators. By and large, the key simulators, that is for example, the tactically engagement simulator, a contract for which has been let, and which we anticipate receiving in service next year, will both enhance the quality of training on Salisbury Plain training area, and in Germany and BATUS, and make it much more realistic and cost-effective, and we will get a far better product through the medium of tactical engagement simulation. So where we lose in some areas we hope that simulation will in-fill and prevent us losing our expertise at brigade and battlefield level.

2258. I am not clear which simulator is called what, but I believe there is a simulator for artillery scheduled for next year?

(Major General McAfee) Yes, that is right. I am not very well briefed on that.

(Colonel Starmer-Smith) There were two sides to the tactical engagement simulation. The first is the direct fire laser system which will be introduced next year, and that contract has been let, and we will have the first models in next year. We are looking at an Area Weapon Effects Simulator (AWES), and that is due in about 1997, and that will simulate the indirect fire aspects of training which we do not have at the moment. That is under consideration, and contracts have not yet been let.

2259. The budgeting for that piece of equipment is something that does come out of the standard training budget?

(Colonel Starmer-Smith) As far as I am aware, Sir, it is within the programme.

(Mr Dreher) It is within the budget, Chairman, and you are quite right that one has to take a view about resources in the round. If the priority is that this has to be funded we shall have to see whether it is affordable and whether something else has to drop off.

2260. Would that be specifically in the training budget?

(Mr Dreher) It would be in the context of the training budget, yes.

(Major General McAfee) Perhaps our biggest concern at the moment is of course the improvements that we need to make to existing Army field training centres, particularly those on Salisbury Plain and Otterburn, because when the Army is largely home-based by 1995, when three-quarters of the Army is stationed in the United Kingdom, I am afraid the infrastructure of those two areas is simply not good enough to absorb the additional training we will need to carry out on them. It is largely an infrastructure problem. It is a question of access roads to allow the access to heavy vehicles and to avoid upsetting or overburdening the local communities. It will be

expensive and I am afraid the costs are not catered for in the transition works funding, so the costs will have to come out of the core programme and we are looking at making a case for that this year, which I think inevitably will go for ministerial submission, and we regard that as our primary concern in Army training, and an area in which we would be very grateful for any support that the Committee might be able to give.

2261. The Committee is very carefully noting what you are saying. If I can cover training lands, the Committee did visit Salisbury and were very well looked after by General Dutton and it is nice to see Colonel Starmer-Smith too here today. The MOD have also recently been examined by the National Audit Office and the Public Accounts Committee on training lands, so I do not want to go over ground which has been fully covered in other reports. Has there been any progress on management, computerisation of booking and quantification of current capacity?

(Major General McAfee) There has indeed, sir, and I think we have been rightly criticised in the past for not having a comprehensive management system to match land holdings against our training needs, and of course for making sure that our estate is no bigger than necessary. We are presently conducting a study to review our future requirement for training land in the United Kingdom and that report will be out by the end of the year. We are also developing a computer model of the Army's training requirement which next year will enable us to match the variables of land availability in terms of size, weather, tourism, farming, all these variables matched against the variables of the training requirement. I hope by installing that at our major training areas we will be able to know exactly who is doing what where and to make sure that the land is being utilised as effectively as possible within those variables. Clearly there never can be 100 per cent use of training land or we would end up with environmental problems, but all these will be taken into account. We have commissioned two environmental impact studies which are presently running and which will report later in the year on Otterburn and Salisbury Plain. Generally in the round I think we could fairly say that the Army training lands is pulling all these requirements together so that we can be more accountable and answer the sort of questions that have been put to us in the past and prove that we have a need for the land that we do indeed hold.

2262. I am not clear whether there is a central training budget or whether each unit has to pay for its own unit budget towards these training costs.

(Mr Dreher) There is basically an overall budget. I do not know whether Colonel Starmer-Smith has more details.

(Colonel Starmer-Smith) The answer, sir, is that for the six Army field training centres I have a central budget which comes eventually from the United Kingdom land forces. I have a central budget which allows me to manage the six Army field training centres and my remit is to provide the facilities for not only the Army but the Air Force and the Navy and the Marines if they are required, so I have a budget to manage those which includes the provision of the ranges, the staffing and everything else.

[**Chairman** *Cont*]

2263. You do not debit a unit who uses it?

(Colonel Starmer-Smith) No, sir. They are not charged. It is my requirement to provide those facilities.

2264. Just two brief questions of detail. First of all, can you tell us where you can fire Rapier?

(Colonel Starmer-Smith) The Hebrides, Sir, is the place where it is done, at the Royal Artillery Range in the Hebrides, and some of the trials are done by the manufacturers at Aberporth in Wales.

2265. And the multi-launch rocket system, the AS90, would that be at Otterburn?

(Colonel Starmer-Smith) The only place where we may fire the practice round for the MLRS on an Army field training centre is at Otterburn where we have one position. We may not fire it on Salisbury Plain because we would be required for safety reasons to close the main road running across Salisbury Plain. We can fire it but with very limited training value at some of the proof and experimental establishments, but it gives us very little training value. That is one of the reasons of course why we are looking at developing Otterburn, so we are capable of taking MLRS firing. AS90 we can at present fire on Salisbury Plain only within the United Kingdom. Again, because of the location of the units in the future we are looking at developing Otterburn to allow us to take AS90 there as well.

2266. Finally, for the TA training, I am not clear whether that is dealt with under an entirely separate system or whether it is an integral part of your overall regular Army training pattern.

(Major General McAfee) It is integral, sir, as far as their Phase 2 training is concerned, which is carried out at arms and service establishments. Phase 2 tends to be done on a TA basis although I confess I am not an expert on the reserve Army. If you have a specific question we will certainly get the answer for you.

2267. I think we will put our specific question in writing rather than detain you. It is the overall planning aspect that concerns me.

(Colonel Starmer-Smith) The collective training strategy and the compendium are applicable to the TA in exactly the same way as they are applicable to the regular Army. They have the same standards. Obviously, we would not expect them to meet the standard or the timeframe in quite the same way as the regular Army would because of the amount of training, but they are offered to them as the same guidelines and package, and they can take what they will out of them. We have been in contact with Commander United Kingdom Field Army who has responsibility for the TA, and he has accepted that.

Chairman: As an ex-TA gunner myself, I was delighted that the TA gunner only regiment fired more rounds last year than any regular regiment. Thank you very much indeed for coming to see us and I hope it was not as terrifying as you indicated on Wednesday it might be.

WEDNESDAY 8 DECEMBER 1993

Members present:

Sir Nicholas Bonsor, in the Chair

Mr Michael Colvin   Mr John Home Robertson
Mr Bruce George   Mr John McWilliam

Examination of Witnesses

MR J MICHAEL MOSS, Assistant Under Secretary (Naval Personnel); REAR ADMIRAL NICHOLAS J WILKINSON, Director General of Naval Manpower and Training; REAR ADMIRAL JEREMY J BLACKHAM, Chief of Staff to the Commander-in-Chief Naval Home Command and REAR ADMIRAL TIMOTHY J ENGLAND, Chief Staff Officer (Support) to the Commander-in-Chief Fleet, examined.

Chairman

275. Good morning, Mr Moss. Can you, for the record, please introduce your team?

(*Mr Moss*) Thank you, Chairman. I am the Assistant Under Secretary (Naval Personnel). On my right is Rear Admiral Nicholas Wilkinson, who is the Director General of Naval Manpower and Training in the Ministry of Defence. On my left, Rear Admiral Jeremy Blackham, who is the Chief of Staff to Commander in Chief Naval Home Command.

276. Thank you very much. Can we start by having a look at the effects of drawdown and initial training. On the Committee's visit to SULTAN and COLLINGWOOD we heard something of the effects of the drawdown on the training system, particularly the big fall in recruitment and the total freeze in some branches. Can you give details, showing the overall picture in terms of the fall in initial training numbers?

(*Mr Moss*) There has certainly been a fall in recruitment, Chairman. For example, the total number of recruits in 1991–92 to the naval service was some 6,500, whereas by the last financial year, 1992–93, it had fallen to just under 2,300. So certainly the numbers have fallen. On the effects on the service, perhaps I could ask Admiral Wilkinson to elaborate.

(*Rear Admiral Wilkinson*) Clearly, with cutbacks like that, both to the recruiting machine and the training machine, they are vastly under-used at the minute. This means that we have had to redeploy many of the staff on to other tasks: on the recruiting side, to looking to the years ahead and when the numbers might go up again, and concentrating on those of a younger age; and on the training machine, partly to updating some of the courses whose course design had fallen behind, and partly to redeploying the instructors and instructing officers to other tasks, such as the many studies which are currently under way to do with the management of change.

277. Does the fall-off in numbers actually mean that you save a substantial sum of money, or are so many of the costs fixed that this is marginal?

(*Rear Admiral Blackham*) Well, Chairman, if I can answer that in two sections: it does, of course, save a substantial amount of money, namely in the pay of the people whom you are not recruiting. That is, perhaps, self-evident; the number of people on the untrained strength comes down quite sharply and so the cost of that untrained strength comes down quite sharply.

Insofar as standards are concerned, our major aim is to fix whatever the steady state level of recruitment ought to be and then adjust the complements and facilities and amenities in those establishments to match precisely that level. We are in something of a dip at the moment. So the costs will come down in terms of running costs and usage, but not in terms of staff, until we can reduce the staff to match whatever the permanent throughput turns out to be.

278. Can you give an indication of when you think you will be able to complete the running down of the staff to match the student intake?

(*Rear Admiral Blackham*) I would hope that as a result of current exercises we would be able to establish what the precise infrastructure and size and shape of the Navy would be, and it would follow from that.

279. What time-scale are you looking at?

(*Rear Admiral Blackham*) We would like to do it as soon as possible.

280. Does that mean a year?

(*Rear Admiral Blackham*) I would hope it would be in less than a year.

281. Can you give any indication of the size of the staff requirement that you envisage?

(*Mr Moss*) Perhaps I could ask Admiral Wilkinson to explain the work that is going on to that end?

(*Rear Admiral Wilkinson*) Perhaps if I can start in recent years, because we have been undertaking a programme of reduction in the training machine for some years now, which started in the mid-1980s. We had 22 training establishments, we are now down to 15 and we intend to be down, on current plans, to 11 by 1998. We have reduced training costs in that period by about 36 per cent in real terms. We also have some establishments currently under closure: the remnants of HMS VERNON, and HMS DAEDALUS which will be combined into SULTAN when DAEDALUS itself is closed. We have recently closed ROYAL ARTHUR and MERCURY. Looking ahead, we set up a few months ago a Training Way Ahead Study to pull together all the disparate elements of change in the training area, with a view to reducing a proportion of the costs spent in this area. This umbrella study will look at, amongst other things, the optimum whole Navy training organisation, including the possibility of a Naval training agency; to look at the future of the HMS DRYAD, School of Maritime Operations; to look at the

[Chairman Cont]

future of initial officer training; the length of our training pipelines; the amount of pre-joining training we do—that is, training before people go to specific ships—the amount of training we do at sea; live gunnery training, and foreign and commonwealth training—amongst other things. This study, as I say, started before the recent announcement on the defence costs study, Frontline First, but is consistent with it. Because there are no sacred cows in any of this work, we may be looking at further reductions below the 11 establishments I have mentioned. If I might end by emphasising we shall be looking in this work at the most cost-effective way of meeting the current standards of operational performance.

282. I think you said you were looking at DRYAD as one of the options. Is DRYAD not an essential part of your training regime?
(Rear Admiral Wilkinson) It certainly is at the minute. What we are looking at (and we are looking at all establishments, as we must do under this study) is whether there is another way of doing the training which is currently undertaken there. If so, in what time-scale.

283. Can we have a look at the initial training of seamen. I believe that after their training at RALEIGH, ratings have an initial sea posting quite soon after. Is that a problem for you, or can you place them quite easily?
(Rear Admiral Wilkinson) There has been a problem of different waiting times. This is caused, really, by the fact that the available ships for the ratings to go to have reduced slightly, whereas the recruiting which we undertook a few years ago, has produced a backlog. This is being rapidly reduced, and we hope that by next year we will be down to a fairly insignificant level.

284. What sort of level would that be—the waiting time?
(Rear Admiral Wilkinson) A matter of weeks rather than months. It is something we are still looking at closely.

285. Hopefully, the "unhappy juniors" referred to by a senior officer in a recent Flag Office surface fleet meeting will be less unhappy next year than they are at the moment.
(Rear Admiral Wilkinson) Hopefully they will be at sea.

286. Can we move on to the study carried out by Sir Michael Layard into naval officer training. Has that been completed?
(Rear Admiral Wilkinson) The study itself has been completed but there is a lot of follow-up work to be done. The study deliberately, in the short time it had, could not complete much of the detailed work which was necessary to make sure that the structures proposed were, in fact, all viable. That work is now under way and there are a number of teams working on various different areas of the report's recommendations. One thing which we shall need to revisit in the light of Frontline First is whether all those recommendations are still valid.

287. Was Manadon, for example, part of the recommendation made?

(Rear Admiral Wilkinson) It was covered in the report but was, in fact, already being studied separately by my own staff beforehand.

288. Can you tell us what the principal changes are that have been recommended?
(Rear Admiral Wilkinson) On Manadon?

289. No, overall.
(Rear Admiral Wilkinson) Overall. There are, I think, about 60 recommendations all together, but the main ones are, for example, moving away from full career commissions (everyone joining on shorter commissions); the abolition of the separate general, supplementary and special duties lists; different patterns of early career and longer career, which are currently under study; different methods of extracting people from the lower deck; slight changes to the promotion system—and there are many others, too.
(Mr Moss) You see, Chairman, it was a study not on training but of the officer structure with training implications, which, as the Admiral says, are being pursued.

290. I see. It was the training implications, obviously, I was getting at principally. Would it be possible for the Committee to see a copy of the report?
(Mr Moss) We could certainly look at that, Chairman. It is quite a weighty report and there was a synopsis prepared, which might be more suitable, but we could take that away.

291. I think we are quite used to reading lengthy reports, Mr Moss, and I would prefer to have that than the synopsis, please. Is your reaction to this report affected strongly by the Frontline First study? In other words, how inherent in Sir Michael's recommendations is the cost factor?
(Mr Moss) There were, of course, cost implications, and I think one would expect some savings to flow from it. Whether the work of Frontline First impinges on the recommendations he made, I cannot guess yet.

292. Coming back to the training point, specifically, is there a danger, do you think, of seamen, engineers, and supply officers, for example, being trained so separately that they lack a cohesive training unit?
(Rear Admiral Wilkinson) There is nothing in the report which will alter the common training that all naval officers will continue to get.

293. Are there any significant recent changes at Dartmouth?
(Rear Admiral Blackham) Perhaps I can answer that, Chairman. Dartmouth is still doing what it has traditionally always done. That is to say, introducing officers to the Navy, providing a common, professional base and developing the qualities which we have always expected of our officers. Of course the training is adjusted from time to time to ensure it remains apposite to the sorts of ships that we have and the sorts of activities that they perform, but fundamentally it remains the same as it always has been. Currently it is 18 weeks' worth of general naval training, followed by a term at sea in the initial training squadron. So I think the general pattern is the same but the detail, as you

[Chairman *Cont]*

would expect, is amended from time to time to reflect what is going on in the real world.

294. Is it the same course for school leavers and graduates? Or do you differentiate?

(Rear Admiral Blackham) The general naval training course is given to everybody.

295. Are you moving towards graduate entry, or are you still looking at having school leavers as well?

(Rear Admiral Wilkinson) Both, but we are looking to increase the proportion of graduates who enter each year. The target is to get up to 70 per cent. In fact, this year, for the first time, we have exceeded that target.

296. Turning to staff colleges, how seriously does the Navy take staff college training?

(Rear Admiral Wilkinson) It is taken seriously, but not all officers who should do it manage to do it. That, I think, is something which the Officer Study Group report has addressed and which we are now looking at further. The reason why some officers who should do it do not is more to do with the speed of moving through the promotion system than any lack of desire on our part to give proper staff training.

297. I believe that in the past sometimes the staff college training has been the final posting of an officer who is about to leave. Is that still the case?

(Rear Admiral Blackham) As an ex-Commandant of the staff college, Chairman, perhaps I can say a word about it. That certainly was not the case in the time I was there, which was the late-1980s. In passing, at that time we trained a higher percentage of naval officers at the staff college than either of the other two services. As Admiral Wilkinson has already explained, the emphasis has always been on the right people but there was an increasing correlation between promotion and appointing to a staff job and undergoing staff training. Certainly I was not asked to take—and would not have taken—people who did not appear to have bright careers ahead of them.

298. It did seem rather a waste. Presumably it must have been some years ago, but it does seem rather a waste of an opportunity.

(Rear Admiral Blackham) It certainly would be, but I am quite certain it does not go on.

299. Thank you. I think it would be helpful if we could have some note of the people who are going through, and the numbers and ranks of people going through, the staff college, if that could be arranged.

(Mr Moss) Certainly, Chairman.

Chairman: Thank you very much. Can we move on to look specifically at Manadon and the consequences of closure there.

Mr Colvin

300. Now that it has been decided that Bachelor of Engineering courses at Manadon are going to cease, there is going to be a sponsored student scheme at Southampton instead. Is that correct?

(Mr Moss) Correct.

301. What drop-out rate is being assumed by the Navy, and under what obligation will graduates be to serve in the Royal Navy (and for how long) when they have completed their courses?

(Rear Admiral Wilkinson) Those who are under training at Southampton University in future will not actually be in the Navy.

302. Not actually be remunerated?

(Rear Admiral Wilkinson) Not actually in the Navy. Our intention is that they will be honorary RNR officers and will be remunerated on that basis, but because they will not be in the Navy they will not have the same return of service commitments as if they were.

303. You have had other sponsored students previously on university courses. What is your experience with them? Have they taught you caution with regard to university courses?

(Rear Admiral Wilkinson) On wastage?

304. Yes.

(Rear Admiral Wilkinson) The wastage of those who have been through university is not markedly different from those who come through other routes. Many of them, of course, joined on short-service commissions anyway in the past.

305. If people do drop out will there be any obligation on them to pay anything back?

(Rear Admiral Wilkinson) I would have to look into that as to exactly what the answer is and give you a follow-up answer on that.

306. Thank you. The Navy is justly proud of its Upper Yardman scheme by which BTEC-qualified ratings can become officers at Manadon and gain a Bachelor of Engineering degree. Will an Upper Yardman have to pass a Southampton test to enter, or just the RN's own internal tests?

(Rear Admiral Wilkinson) The Southampton interview as well, yes.

307. What will become of the Instructor Branch, following the rundown of Manadon?

(Rear Admiral Wilkinson) The future of the Instructor Branch is not dependent directly on the future of Manadon; that is something which has been assessed by the Officer Study Group and is still under study as to whether there *will* be an Instructor Branch in future at all.

308. Is the investigation of Manadon also looking at the Royal Corps of Naval Constructors, because that too I believe is very dependent on Manadon?

(Rear Admiral Wilkinson) Yes.

309. What will be the effect on that?

(Rear Admiral Wilkinson) The DES are currently going through Manadon and they are considering what their alternative arrangement will be.

Mr Home Robertson

310. If I may cut in, at least to come back to this question of the students at Southampton University, what does it cost to put a student through one of these courses?

(Rear Admiral Wilkinson) We shall be paying them £1,200 a year as a bursary.

[Mr Home Robertson *Cont]*

311. Are you paying anything to the university?
(Rear Admiral Wilkinson) No, because they will be LEA-sponsored students.

312. They are LEA-funded, are they?
(Rear Admiral Wilkinson) Yes.

313. Will some of them have student loans?
(Rear Admiral Wilkinson) Presumably, yes.

314. You have confirmed, though, that there is no specific obligation on them to come into the Navy or to do any form of service in the Navy?
(Rear Admiral Wilkinson) They will not have the same obligation as if they were naval officers already, yes.

Chairman

315. It does not appear, Admiral, that they will have any obligation, will they, under this system?
(Rear Admiral Wilkinson) They will have, we hope, a wish to enter the Navy[1].

316. A wish and an obligation are two very different things.
(Rear Admiral Wilkinson) Indeed, yes. Of course, we shall be sponsoring too, so there will be a repayment of sponsorship if they decide to drop out.

317. The sponsorship is £1,200 a year?
(Rear Admiral Wilkinson) Yes.

318. So they will have £3,600 out of the Navy?
(Rear Admiral Wilkinson) Yes.

319. What is to stop a young man saying, "This is great fun, I'll take £3,600 for three years and then go and use my engineering degree somewhere else"?
(Rear Admiral Wilkinson) It is a risk with all sponsored students.

320. I think that many of them have to pay it back. Certainly they do under the Army scheme.
(Rear Admiral Wilkinson) They would have to repay the sponsorship, yes.

321. They would have to?
(Rear Admiral Wilkinson) Yes.

322. Are you sure about that?
(Rear Admiral Wilkinson) Indeed, yes.

Mr George

323. Manadon is a fine site and wonderful real estate for somebody with a desire to flog it off and make money. Would you give us assurances that the rationale for closing the place down was other than gaining money for the Ministry of Defence?
(Mr Moss) The rationale, Mr George, for changing the training scheme for engineer officers reflects the Navy's requirement—down to some 30 a year to be trained at Manadon for the engineering specialisation in

the Royal Navy, in addition to the engineering officers we draw direct from university. So needs must. Under those circumstances, one could not run Manadon to train 30 engineer officers a year.

324. I am sure we shall come back to that in a moment. My second question is, what sort of testing did you do at Southampton University to ensure or to guarantee that the courses provided there are at least as good as those provided at Manadon? Are the academics specialists in those areas where specialisms are found in Manadon?
(Rear Admiral Wilkinson) Yes. We looked at many other universities besides Southampton. We chose Southampton as being a university which already had all the kinds of courses we needed, and because Southampton is moving to a modular system we are able, by choosing the right modules, to produce a package with Southampton which is entirely appropriate to our sub-specialisations amongst engineers (in other words, marine engineering, weapon engineering and aero engineering).

Mr Home Robertson

325. Perhaps I may pursue one further point about who is paying for this specialist education which has hitherto been dealt with by the Ministry of Defence, has it not?
(Rear Admiral Wilkinson) Yes.

326. We are talking about how many students per year going in?
(Rear Admiral Wilkinson) About 30 a year.

327. They hitherto have been paid for by the Ministry of Defence, and that responsibility has been unloaded onto the local education authorities, you are saying?
(Rear Admiral Wilkinson) Correct.

328. As far as you are aware, has any extra allocation gone into that budget for that purpose?
(Rear Admiral Wilkinson) I am not aware of any extra allocation.
Mr Home Robertson: I think it is most unlikely. Thank you.

Mr Colvin

329. Given the likelihood that RNEC will close, what about all the other courses, short and long? By removing the Bachelor of Engineering course do not you effectively pull the plug on all the others too?
(Rear Admiral Wilkinson) We are looking at the others. For example, some courses might be done at Southampton, others might be done at Shrivenham which we are already using for other postgraduate courses. The BA degree which we have been running at Manadon for a number of years we have decided to put on ice for the time being, because we are already achieving our target of 70 per cent graduates direct from universities.

330. I gather that you will be transferring application training to SULTAN and COLLINGWOOD?
(Rear Admiral Wilkinson) Yes.

---

[1] In the selection of candidates for sponsorship, the Royal Navy will pay particular attention to the evidence of motivation to join the service. Retention of a candidate's sponsorship, once granted, will be kept under continuous review.

[Mr Colvin Cont]

331. Will there be additional costs in that, and are there advantages or drawbacks in so doing?

(Rear Admiral Blackham) I am not sure that we have got quite to the position that you suggest, so obviously we are looking at how we might produce what we call "application training" (that is to say, the turning of a degree in engineering into practising engineering). Clearly, SULTAN and COLLINGWOOD are places well equipped to do that. The final decision will depend on an investment appraisal which will show where we get the best training for the best price. You may be right, SULTAN will be the best place, and if it is it will be because it has been proved to be the most cost-effective place to do it.

332. Will Operations Branch officers have access to university-level engineering training?

(Rear Admiral Blackham) Officers of Seamen Branch, for example?

333. Yes.

(Rear Admiral Blackham) At the moment they do through the normal university entry schemes which are applicable to them. That will continue.

334. We were talking about costs earlier, but can we look at the question of capital receipts from the sale of the Manadon site? I understand that there are some quite important buildings there. There is a tithe barn and a chapel which may be listed. What scope is there for capital receipts? Will there merely have to be transfers of capital from one part of the budget to another when you know what needs to be sold?

(Mr Moss) The possible proceeds of sale would come into the investment appraisal which is examining the future of the existing training and the future of the site and so on.

335. But in the case of the Royal William Yard which was sold, you had to transfer money to a potential buyer to enable them to buy it. What will happen with the Manadon site?

(Mr Moss) It is too early to say, Mr Colvin.

(Rear Admiral Blackham) There is no sign, from the informal contacts which I have had, that it is likely to a buyer. What we were looking at with the Royal William Yard was a very large building, a very large estate almost, which has many listed buildings within the estate. My understanding at any rate, from the informal contacts which I have had, is that the Manadon site is not proving likely to deter a buyer at the moment.

336. Would it be possible for us to see the investment appraisal figures?

(Mr Moss) They are not ready yet.

337. When they are, could we see them?

(Mr Moss) By all means, we could report to you.

338. In 1966 the Howard-English Report recommended that the Royal Navy's Department of Nuclear Science and Technology and its mini-reactor JASON should move to Manadon. That is a recommendation which was repeated later and then accepted in 1989, but it has not actually happened, so what is going to happen, as far as that is concerned?

(Mr Moss) Obviously, you are quite right, it was announced in 1989 that the department and JASON would move to Manadon. Clearly, we are having to look at that again, and so for the time being it will remain at Greenwich. The study which Admiral Wilkinson has outlined will perhaps steer us to the fate of JASON and the Department of Nuclear Science and Technology.

339. How can you best provide all Royal Naval engineer officers with some nuclear engineering options, with the added benefit of eventually shortening the period required for specialised nuclear propulsion-powered training? You mentioned Shrivenham earlier. Is there any possibility that Shrivenham might be able to help?

(Rear Admiral Wilkinson) We are looking at not so much Shrivenham but the university sector to see if there is any scope there.

340. The university sector generally?

(Rear Admiral Wilkinson) Yes.

341. Do you have any particular universities in mind?

(Rear Admiral Wilkinson) I do not have details here, I am afraid.

Mr Colvin: Thank you.

Chairman: Can I ask John Home Robertson to take us on and look at individual, units and formation training.

Mr Home Robertson

342. Having qualified initially, what form of annual testing of a sailor's skills is there? Do sailors, for example, take regular firearms tests, or do they just take tests connected with their particular branch of the service?

(Mr Moss) I think that, as with any educational institution, one finds conventional things like examinations and continuous assessment. No doubt Admiral Blackham will elaborate on that in a moment. As far as firearms are concerned, they all receive safety and accuracy training as part of their initial training, and then testing and continuation training depends on whether they are required to bear arms in the course of their duties.

343. So what you are saying is that it is only if it is specifically required that they will be expected to do it?

(Mr Moss) Yes, later on.

344. What about first aid? Is that done repeatedly?

(Rear Admiral Blackham) Perhaps I could help. Within establishments themselves every training session, as you would expect, has a quality assurance element to ensure that the training we are giving relates directly to the operational performance standards demanded by C in C Fleet. As Mr Moss has said, during the progress of any particular course students will be continuously assessed and examined at the end of it. Amongst the things which are mandatory before going to sea in a ship are firefighting and damage control training and first aid training. There is a school at HMS RALEIGH and a school at Portsmouth which conduct that training. People are required to pass those

[Mr Home Robertson Cont]

courses before they can go to their first sea draft. Thereafter, once ratings get into ships, they are almost universally required to complete task books which confirm the training they have had and prepare them for further advancement. The normal progress would be to complete a task book and then return to the training school for a formal course before advancement. So there is a continual process which goes on both at sea and ashore, and they feed into each other.

345. There is a continual training process on all these key subjects, but is there a continual assessment and repeated testing?
(Rear Admiral Blackham) I think there is continual assessment at sea. You are talking now about skills, or firefighting and first aid?

346. About the whole range of skills and specialities.
(Mr Moss) May I call on Rear Admiral England, who is the Chief Staff Officer (Support) to the Commander in Chief Fleet, to answer that.
(Rear Admiral England) You have heard more about individual training so far. By the time the individual comes to the fleet, whether it be in a surface ship, a submarine or a small ship, now we are talking about unit or formation training, and all that starts with our work-up organisation.

347. I want to concentrate on individual training.
(Rear Admiral England) Then you are back with the Commander in Chief Naval Home Command!

348. There was a skilful attempt to pass the buck there!
(Rear Admiral Blackham) I do not think so. I thought you were talking about seagoing duty.

349. I want to focus on the training of individual sailors. What I think we have now established is that people are repeatedly assessed and tested to ensure that they keep up the standard of skills on essential parts of their job?
(Rear Admiral Blackham) Yes. I think that we have described what happens in the shore service and what happens at sea. On the specific skills you mentioned, such as first aid, firearms and firefighting, they are generally required to get them before going to sea on their first draft.

350. Is there an annual personal fitness test for seamen?
(Rear Admiral Blackham) This has been a subject of debate over the years, and at times there has been and at times there has not.

351. Is there one now?
(Rear Admiral Blackham) There is not currently, I think I am right in saying.
(Rear Admiral Wilkinson) There is not a compulsory one.

352. That is a major distinction from the Army where we were told that everybody had to go through it—officers, men, women. It is a softer life in the Navy, is it?
(Rear Admiral Blackham) I think the fitness has to suit the job in hand. Certainly at basic training establishments training in fitness is a vital part of the whole course.

Chairman

353. Presumably an admiral of a ship, if he felt so inclined, could insist on his crew meeting his own criteria in that regard?
(Rear Admiral Blackham) He certainly could, yes.

354. Would he, and do many do so, as far as you are aware?
(Rear Admiral Blackham) I can only speak from my own experience. I have never felt it necessary to do that. In fact, my point of view is that with a group of young, active and by definition spirited people it is not really necessary, there is a great deal of exercise going on. In my last command on ARK ROYAL I found that the flight deck was full at almost every moment with people running around, and I felt that there was enough exercise going on to make *me* tired at any rate!

355. I would have thought even in the Navy there are bound to be one or two who would be less inclined to do that.
(Rear Admiral Blackham) Indeed.

356. You would not have felt that they needed to be chased up?
(Rear Admiral Blackham) I would certainly have been aware and would have expected my team to be aware of—if I may put it in this rather untidy way—the physical condition of people who worked for them and made judgements about whether they were fit to do their job or not. Certainly, for example, obesity is a reason why a man might be warned for discharge or not promoted. Medical examination is a compulsory feature, I think I am right in saying, in any advancement.
Mr Home Robertson: It is very insensitive to talk about obesity in this Committee!
Mr George: Or emaciation!

Mr Home Robertson

357. You seem to be suggesting that there used to be such a regular fitness test, which must have been dropped at some stage.
(Rear Admiral Blackham) There was a period when a test was introduced. I am not sure I am sufficiently informed to answer. I know there were problems with it, not least the sudden introduction of compulsory testing leading to people actually—in one or two cases-suffering fatal accidents as a consequence of the test. I hasten to add that was probably not because they were overweight but because they had other congenital defects which were exacerbated. I am not actually, from my own experience, able to give enough detail on that.

358. When was it dropped?
(Rear Admiral Wilkinson) I think they tried it twice. I cannot remember the years, I am afraid.

Chairman

359. I think it would be interesting to have a note on the periods that it was introduced and any reasons anybody may be aware of as to why it was dropped.

[**Chairman** *Cont*]

(*Rear Admiral Wilkinson*) This year we have introduced a voluntary fitness test, and this may well lead—when people get used to the idea—to a compulsory fitness test, as some people would like. At the minute it is voluntary and, as I say, has just been reintroduced.

(*Rear Admiral England*) If I could point out, one of the practical problems of introducing any form of test is that you need facilities to test, and for the large majority of our people in ships, submarines and small ships (with the exception of the ARK ROYALs and INVINCIBLEs of this world, who have a flight deck) it is impossible to test anybody—rating or officer—at sea for physical fitness. So we encourage them to actually keep fit but testing them for fitness is not practical.

360. People are not at sea for twelve months of the year.

(*Rear Admiral England*) They are either at sea or on leave, or they are needed to work. The ability of the Navy to have facilities around them on a regular basis for physical fitness training and testing is difficult, as you can appreciate.

361. You have told us in the past about the introduction of the CAPES system into the Fleet intended to be complete by the end of 1993 (that means, I think, within the next two or three weeks) "based on a range of ship-based Performance Indicators, the system measures manning, equipment availability and the levels of collective and individual training achieved". (That was taken from the SDE 92 Report in evidence that was given to the Committee.) How do you measure ship training achievements?

(*Rear Admiral Blackham*) I think I can pass the buck there!

(*Rear Admiral England*) Can I give you a general answer and then move into the CAPES area, because they are two quite separate questions? Initially, as I was beginning to explain, once the trained individual comes to a ship, or submarine (whatever its size or shape), then you are talking about unit training. That unit training is undertaken initially through our sea training organisations—Flag Officer Sea training, command submarine sea training and the small ships organisation. They set the definitive standards for unit training. So that by the time the ship or submarine emerges from that period of training we have taken the individual skills of the Commander-in-Chief Naval Home Command and we have moulded them into a total unit which is capable of looking after itself and carrying out its functions, whatever they may be. Those units then perform other exercises, where they move into groups and join maritime exercises, either national or NATO exercises, where they are then trained and experienced in a group formation. There is intensive assessment of the ship or the submarine during its operational sea training period, normally about six weeks for a surface ship and a similar time for a submarine, where they have staff who are specially trained and deployed for that purpose, looking over their shoulders for 24 hours a day. That is the most intensive assessment period. That is something different from CAPES, which I will come on to in a minute. Once the ship emerges into operational time, then the assessment is more subjective than objective

and there are visiting teams of experts associated with the various commands within the Fleet who visit the ship periodically and make assessments. If there are any areas felt inadequate they target that area. The CAPES system is now widely deployed in most surface ships, most small ships and a large number of submarines. That is a computer-based assessment system whereby a lot of information is fed in on a regular basis by the ship or submarine staff, running through from the technical situation within the ship to the standards of training and the number of exercises—both individual weapon systems and multi-ship exercises—they have done. Through the numerical assessment there is then a print-out, as it were, as to what standard that ship has achieved or not achieved. The efficiency of CAPES is, obviously, taking time to assess. We know what it indicated last week, we know what it is indicating this week, and we can see whether it is going up or down against the criteria we have set, but it will take a little more experience before we can say that if a ship reads 8, or whatever it is, on the scale it is acceptable for this or that sort of deployment.

362. It sounds like an awful lot of paper!

(*Rear Admiral England*) Funnily enough, less paper than there used to be.

363. I am glad to hear that. Is it a collective assessment, based on all the individual scores and coming out at a collective, overall assessment of the quality of the ship and its crew?

(*Rear Admiral England*) Yes. You can take any level. You can look at, not quite an individual person but you can certainly look at an individual system, and assess it in terms of its material and people availabilities and know what standard has been reached. Or you can take the composite of all the various systems in the ship or submarine and get a read-out for the state of that ship as a whole.

364. But you can have a close look at the gunnery, the radar, the sonar and everything else individually and then identify that. Do the weapons systems actually have to be used at stated intervals?

(*Rear Admiral England*) Yes, they do, and that is laid down and is part of the criteria that feeds into CAPES.

365. And it is happening?

(*Rear Admiral England*) Indeed.

(*Rear Admiral Blackham*) It may be helpful to say that, for example, in ARK ROYAL's Adriatic deployment (and I imagine this is common on all ships) all our weapons systems were run through every day. That is to say, run through up to the point, of course, of actually discharging a missile—which, in a way is the least important part of the system because you can measure its performance and parameters without actually doing that. That happened on a daily and, even, on a watch basis.

366. You mentioned smaller ships. What about RFAs?

(*Rear Admiral England*) They have a similar system now, although their crews are civilian, by definition.

367. So all ships are covered?

(*Rear Admiral England*) RFAs go through the Portland system.

[Chairman *Cont*]

368. Under this system do you have training levels which are laid down and actually enforced, so that if something is lacking there is a mechanism to make sure standards are brought up?

(Rear Admiral England) Yes. There are what are called Fleet Charge Documents that lay down the sort of pattern of training, of exercises, of weapon firing, which are supposedly undertaken by each ship or each type of system, and the ship is required to report through the CAPES system now (it used to be a paper system) how often and whether they have achieved those assessments, and the regularity of them. If they do not achieve them there could be a good reason—they could be deployed in an area where there is no range or no facility. Then they have to catch up or explain that they feel they are capable of missing out that particular firing.

369. There is one point I wanted to follow up on that. This sounds absolutely marvellous! You are telling us there is continuous assessment going on and everybody is trained and tested, and everything is tip-top. This is difficult to reconcile with the picture of a rather overstretched force that we get. Are you really telling us that everybody in the Navy, however busy they may be in the Adriatic or anywhere else, with special tasks or deployments, is managing to keep up with the whole range of skills?

(Rear Admiral England) They all have the same tasks to achieve. As I say, depending on where they are and what their situation is, they may or may not be achievable. What we can assess is that the ships which are deployed to the more intensive, operational areas—the high-level directed tasks—are achieving all the criteria that are necessary in that area. It may be that a ship which is deployed as the West Indies guard ship may not be achieving all of the capabilities all of the time, but if she is redeployed we make sure that she gets a special weapons training period to increase the skills in those necessary areas.

Chairman

370. You mentioned, Admiral Blackham, that in the Adriatic you were testing up to the point of firing every day. Clearly they cannot fire a missile while they are out on operational exercises, but how often does a ship get the chance to actually fire a missile in its training rota?

(Rear Admiral Blackham) There would be regulations laid down in the same document that Admiral England referred to. I am sure they outline the regularity of fire, but there are rules laid down which say how often it must occur.

Chairman: The Committee would very much like to see a copy of that document. I appreciate it may be classified and it will go through the classified system for examination.

Mr McWilliam

371. Has there been any change in the frequency of laid-down firings over the last ten years? If so, when and what was it? If you cannot tell us we would appreciate a note.

(Rear Admiral Blackham) I am not able to say. My last ship was in date for firings, in accordance with the instructions.

372. Can you say in open session whether or not there has been any change?

(Rear Admiral Blackham) I do not know the answer to that.

(Rear Admiral England) I do not think there has been any substantial change. There is obviously continuous change when we bring in new systems and you change the criteria for that system. Equally, systems that are already in service are reviewed. If I could explain, there are three main reasons for firing of, say, a missile system. One is to train people—that is the ultimate test. One is to prove the system—that is the ultimate test of the system. The third and important reason, of course, is to develop the knowledge of the missile system itself. Where you have a complex missile, a lot of firings occur early in its life, both as trial firing and then firing as part of the training of the ship, during which you develop the envelope of the missile system. Through life you start to drop down on the firings; you know all about the weapon system so the firings get less. So there is a progressive change to the firing pattern, but most systems retain the same basic firing pattern that is laid down at the beginning of their life, and I am not aware of any significant change or intended change outside of those criteria.

Mr Home Robertson

373. We heard in April about the reduction in 1992–93 in exercise commitments "as a result mainly of cuts in fuel". (That was Rear Admiral Abbott.) He said the constraints in 1993–94 looked worse. How is that turning out in practice?

(Mr Moss) I believe, Mr Home Robertson, that no exercises are likely to be cancelled in 1994 because of fuel or costs or ammunition constraints. Perhaps Admiral England would say whether I am right.

(Rear Admiral England) Obviously we review annually the commitments that we can undertake for the next year against our knowledge of our budgets—our resources. As far as the planned activity for this current year, 1993–94, is concerned, there have been no changes forced upon us by constraints.

374. But, presumably, you knew last year what your allocation was going to be. Are you telling us in code that there has still been a further reduction in the amount of exercising possible because of these constraints?

(Rear Admiral England) If I can put it that had we had all the fuel in the world we would have done more, yes. What I am also saying is that we have met our essential and our highly desirable commitments this year.

375. Was there less exercising this year than last year due to fuel?

(Rear Admiral England) No, there has been more this year than last year, in fact. We had an increase in fuel this year.

376. How much of an increase in fuel?

(Rear Admiral England) I think we are about 5 to 10 per cent better off than we were last year.

377. Can you explain how the fuel allocation system operates, in practice, as a constraint on training and

[Mr Home Robertson *Cont*]

exercising? Do ships go to sea with their tanks half full?

(Rear Admiral England) They have a tendency to flip over, if you do that. The system is that we know, broadly speaking, as we plan the operational programme for the year, what fuel allocations we are going to have. We have other factors to take into account because money is also required, for instance, for port visits and for various costs that a ship or submarine incurs as it travels the world. We take all those into account and then we produce what is called the fleet operational programme which specifies what every ship and every submarine is going to be doing on a quarter-day basis. So we know that a ship may be exercising in the morning, on passage in the afternoon, and we can then allocate fuel to that ship based on that pattern of deployment. If it is an exercise where it is likely to have to be dashing around then it is going to have a high fuel allocation. We therefore know quite predictably the sort of fuel consumption we are going to require over at least a year or so, in broad terms, and three months in greater detail. We monitor that fuel consumption. The ships and submarines report to us their fuel uptake each month and, therefore, we can make adjustments, if necessary, to keep it within our allocations.

378. You mentioned submarines. Presumably nuclear fuel does not come into this.

(Rear Admiral England) Exactly.

379. Are we talking about a restriction on the operational hours of engines?

(Rear Admiral England) Not for fuel reasons. We do have, occasionally, operating restrictions on some of our gas turbine engines for other reasons—that is for technical reasons.

380. Is there a restriction on the speed at which ships can travel?

(Rear Admiral England) No, although obviously they are encouraged to travel slowly, and therefore if they are on a passage where they are planning to take twelve hours and can——

381. Run up a sail, or something!

(Rear Admiral England) We have not tried that yet!

(Rear Admiral Blackham) It is quite an appealing idea!

(Rear Admiral England) Obviously ships' commanding officers are encouraged to aim for maximum efficiency where they can, but equally they are not constrained where they need to use fuel for operational reasons.

382. Does that constrain the exercising with weapons, as the Chairman has already mentioned such exercises?

(Rear Admiral England) No, because, as I say, that pattern of activity is predicted and known when we make the original allocations.

383. So if you want to do live firing of depth charges, you can use fuel in order to steer free of the area?

(Rear Admiral England) I do not think we have any live firing of depth charges.

(Rear Admiral Blackham) Again, during my time on ARK ROYAL I never found that fuel was a constraint on anything I wanted to do.

Mr George

384. On the question of recruitment and training, I recall one of the first of the spectacular own-goals by witnesses to this Committee was the civil servant who said, "I may be rather old fashioned about these things, but I still think a woman's place is in the home." Now women are to be found in the Royal Navy, have any evaluations been done on performance and reaction to training (often or usually very sophisticated training)? Has the faith in those who were politically correct been entirely vindicated?

(Mr Moss) Perhaps I could ask Admiral Wilkinson to start on that.

(Rear Admiral Wilkinson) A couple of years ago we invited the University of Plymouth to do an evaluation for us. They recently reported and concluded that integration as a process is working well but unevenly. That tallied very much with our own assessment that, considering the fact that women first went to sea only in September 1990, we have achieved quite a lot in a short time, but there have been some additional management problems some of which we foresaw and some of which we did not. The Plymouth University report suggested certain things we needed to look at some of which we were aware of already and others of which we are now doing. These include such things as looking at other services who employ women and other countries and other civilian organisations too who have large numbers of women employees; improving our own in-service monitoring of progress and spreading internal good practice; improving the management and leadership training which we give to middle-ranking officers and senior ratings in the different ways of dealing with men and women, which many of the men who have been in the service some time are not used to; improving the somewhat chauvinistic attitude of some of the young people who join the service, attitudes they bring with them from civilian life; and things like improving the training we give not only to women but to many men these days whose upper body strength is not as good as it used to be in the handling of heavy objects. So all of those are things which we now have already put in hand to improve. As far as actual personal experience of having women under command at sea is concerned, Admiral Blackham, of course, having come from ARK ROYAL, has just that.

(Rear Admiral Blackham) Yes, Chairman, at the risk of being in Mr George's politically correct group—I am not sure whether that is a compliment or not!—I must say that on ARK ROYAL there were about 120 Wrens. I was about to tell you that you could not very easily tell which was which, but I am sure that was not the case! What I meant to say was that there was no discernible difference in performance. Indeed, interestingly, the women on board, when it came to tackling their task books, typically completed them in about two-thirds of the time that the men took, but they had of course had exactly the same training, and indeed they have been trained in mixed classes throughout their time in the Navy. There was absolutely no professional difficulty at all. There were women in

[**Mr George** *Cont*]

every branch, during my time on ARK ROYAL, except for cooks, believe it or not. In every other branch there were women and, without exception, they performed at least to the standards which the men set. I have a suspicion actually that they dragged the men's standards up with them.

385. Then the Royal Navy has risen to meet the challenge?

(Rear Admiral Blackham) I am sure you would not expect me to comment!

(Rear Admiral England) I am sure I second that.

386. I shall not be even more politically correct and ask about the performance of black women sailors; that would be taking it too far! I would hope that this study could be made available to us in full—not just the summary—because this is obviously a very, very important aspect of recruitment and training. On the question of operational sea training, sea training is to move from Portland to Devonport. When the decision was made there were a number of doubts and uncertainties perhaps which have remained. May I ask a number of questions consequent upon this? Have decisions been taken on the reprovided facilities, including for fixed and rotary wing support, and shore accommodation?

(Rear Admiral England) Yes, the study is well advanced. There is a small team set up under a captain RN who has half a dozen people working for him now, based in Plymouth, who are masterminding the transfer not only of the Flag Officer Sea Training to Plymouth but also the residual closures at Portland which are necessary from the same tasking we have. That study and the implementation of the particular removal of Flag Officer Sea Training to Devonport is going well. We have had one or two moments where we thought we might have difficulties. One was a surveillance radar system which would be needed in the Plymouth area to conduct FOST operations safely. That now looks more likely to be achieved in the right timescale than it did a few months ago. Otherwise it is going extremely well, both the planning and the execution, with a target date of mid-1995 to begin training in Devonport.

387. Thank you. Portland is an excellent facility much used and much admired by foreign navies. When I visit foreign navies they are often eulogistic about the facilities which were provided there. Was there any consultation with NATO navies, or with NATO or SHAPE, or whoever, on the transfer of such facilities to Devonport?

(Rear Admiral England) There has certainly been consultation, through the implementation phase, as to what the facilities will be and how particularly the Dutch and the Germans, who are our two main customers, will interface with it. They are both stated to be very content with the arrangements which we are planning.

388. I understand that there is only going to be one dedicated Sea Training berth at Devonport compared to over 10 at Portland. Accepting the fact that NATO navies are getting smaller almost more quickly than ours is, will that one dedicated berth be sufficient at Devonport?

(Rear Admiral England) I think you are probably talking about buoy berthing as opposed to alongside berthing. There is far more alongside berthing at Devonport available to the ships, of course, than there is at Portland. As far as buoys and staying at sea, in that sense, are concerned, there will be additional buoyage put into the Sound. That is being negotiated at the moment, and that should be adequate for the number of ships we are anticipating receiving there at any one time.

389. Have decisions been taken on the provision of acoustic, magnetic ranges and calibration facilities? Can you assure is unequivocally that there will be no worse facilities than at or off Portland?

(Rear Admiral England) The range facilities off Portland are more associated with the underwater research establishment which is at Portland, and not the activities which are being transferred of Flag Officer Sea Training facilities, so those ranges are not required for operational sea training. We are still looking at whether we need them at all, or whether they should be transferred from there or left there, but they are not part of operational sea training.

390. Why might we not need those facilities?

(Rear Admiral England) The number of ships and submarines we have which require that sort of range are reducing, and we have facilities in other places.

391. As we are getting out of the submarine business, there is less requirement. Has a replacement for the Lulworth Cove range been found yet?

(Rear Admiral England) That is out of my court, I am afraid.

(Rear Admiral Blackham) Lulworth, it has been pointed out to me, is an Army range. I know that we are investigating the provision of a naval gunfire range in that part of the world, but I am not up to date enough to answer your question.

392. Perhaps you will give us a note. Will any alternative be as accessible, given that areas around Plymouth are busy with commercial shipping? Perhaps it might be possible to tell us that also?

(Mr Moss) By all means, yes.

393. The longer transit time means fewer "blocks" of time at sea, reduced perhaps by 25 per cent, and made up in part by fewer harbour days. Could you comment upon that?

(Rear Admiral England) We are looking at the whole modus operandi, if I can call it that, of how we will operate particularly the surface ships in Plymouth. Because it will not be so easy to return to harbour on completion of a training, we think we shall do much more of the staff transferring at sea, within the exercise areas, as opposed to returning to shore. We are looking at the various options, through an investment appraisal, as to whether that helicopter transfer is best done through our own military means or through a commercial contract.

Chairman

394. Before you move on, can I explain that you mentioned the radar problems which you were going to have. How are you setting about solving those?

[**Chairman** *Cont*]

(*Rear Admiral England*) The intention is to have a surface and air surveillance radar situated in HMS Cambridge which is out on the peninsula on the east side of Plymouth. The difficulty has been whether there will be planning application opposition to that sort of radar. It is quite a large domed radar with a golfball on top. The latest indications from consultations which have been taking place are that the South Hams Council will not object, so we hope that is going forward now.

395. It would be critical if it did.

(*Rear Admiral England*) There are other sites which are within Ministry of Defence property—sorry, it is all Ministry of Defence property, but less sensitive ecologically—which could have been used but which would not have been ideal.

Chairman: Because probably anybody thinking of objecting did not hear that.

Mr George

396. We are told that the regular "Thursday war" will continue, but what will be the operational effect of this reduced sea time?

(*Rear Admiral England*) In terms of the amount of time the ships will have on range, as it were, the indications are that we can overcome that, as I say, by transferring staff at sea by helicopter as opposed to bringing the ships back into Plymouth Sound.

397. What is the cost of that?

(*Rear Admiral England*) That is all part of the investment appraisal and comes well within the figures which were originally estimated when we proposed this scheme.

398. Will the move affect the costs of sea training, or the number of ships per week which can be handled by Flag Officer Sea Training?

(*Rear Admiral England*) No, the remit is in fact to rearrange Portland's training at Devonport to cater for exactly the same throughput of ships as there was intended to be at Portland. I am sorry if that is a bit convoluted, but the answer is no.

Mr George: Thank you.

Chairman: Perhaps Mr Home Robertson could lead us into submarine training.

Mr Home Robertson

399. Now that the Upholder submarines have been transferred to the second-hand submarine showroom, I presume there is going to be an increased load on SSNs for various training tasks, for basic training at sea, for Perisher training, for ASW training for our and Allied helicopters, Nimrods and for surface ships. What options are you exploring to avoid either a degradation in RN training (and I understand that there are already reports of a shortfall in the number of submarines being made available for ASW training for our Sea Kings), or alternatively an unacceptable drain on availability of SSNs for operational tasking?

(*Rear Admiral England*) If I could start with Portland, a lot of our training in ASW, of course, goes back to that basic operational sea training period I mentioned earlier, where we have used traditionally a large number of submarines. There is what is called a

Portland credit scheme whereby particularly the Dutch and the German ships which operate and accept our training at Portland do not pay for it in cash terms, they pay for it in kind, and that kind has inevitably been SSK submarine time. So the intention is, and the planning on the move to Devonport is based on this, to use that credit scheme, probably not having an SSK available throughout the working period (in other words, every week of the year that Portland and Devonport were open), but moving towards a scheme where we have a submarine—probably a Dutch or a German one—two out of three weeks, and arranging the training with no detriment to that training, so that we concentrate ASW activities into those two weeks when we have an SSK available. There will also be additional time provided by SSNs in the deeper water, which we can access better from Devonport than we can from Portland, to make up the difference. In non-sea training periods, then we have traditionally had a good rapport with our allies—our NATO allies—in particular, over the use of their submarines when they come into national and NATO exercises. So we see no significant change, although obviously the lack of our own SSKs will reduce the submarine numbers, to some extent.

400. Clearly. You mention the Dutch and the Germans. Are there any other specific navys that we are doing this bartering with?

(*Rear Admiral England*) There is quite a dialogue going on with a number of countries at the moment—I cannot list all of them—to do with our own operational sea training facilities—whether they be at Portland or Devonport in due course, because they are world-known as the best in the world. Even the Americans are thinking of sending us a ship.

401. The French?

(*Rear Admiral England*) Yes, that is a possibility, although we do not, as it were, operate directly with them. We have a lot of mutual co-operation.

402. Broadly speaking, what you are saying is that the Portland credit system—the bartering—should be able to ensure that all those we have been talking about, the Nimrods, surface ships and helicopters, will have as much scope for training with SSKs as in the past.

(*Rear Admiral England*) As they need, is the key. During that period of time when we are undergoing that very intensive training period, yes.

403. You are not paying directly, except as an honest barter.

(*Rear Admiral England*) It is a barter system.

404. Is there a value that you can put on that barter? Does it go through the books at all?

(*Rear Admiral England*) Yes, there is a laid-down criterion, as it were. If we undertake an operational training period with one ship, that buys us a certain amount of days or weeks of SSK time from that particular country. It is laid down quite clearly what the equation is.

405. It may be interesting to get a very brief note on how that works. It sounds interesting.

THE DEFENCE COMMITTEE

25

8 *December 1993*]
Mr J Michael Moss, Rear Admiral Nicholas J Wilkinson,
Rear Admiral Jeremy J Blackham and Rear Admiral Timothy J England
[*Continued*

[**Mr Home Robertson** *Cont*]

(*Mr Moss*) It does not go through the appropriation account[2]. A log is kept and the provision of time by a vessel is assessed and logged. Our aim in the operation of the scheme is to make sure that it breaks even over time.

406. Mutual back-scratching!

(*Mr Moss*) But measured. It works very successfully.

(*Rear Admiral England*) It has been in operation for a number of years.

407. That was not meant to sound derogatory; it sounds eminently sensible. Is there anything else you can use, like remote propelled vehicles, small commercial submarines?

(*Rear Admiral England*) There are various options for using buoy systems and artificial targets, as it were. We are looking at the possibility of some sort of training submarine but that depends on the availability of resources.

Mr Home Robertson: I bet it does!

Mr Colvin

408. As far as the Fleet Air Arm is concerned, can our witnesses tell us what are the principal constraints on Fleet Air Arm training? You will remember, it could be fuel, engine hours, spares availability, environmental restrictions—and others. Or perhaps there are none.

(*Rear Admiral England*) I am not quite sure what you are looking at, Mr Colvin. We plan our training against the resources available in terms of the air crew, the number of trainees coming through, and, of course, like the other areas we have heard about earlier, we have less trainees coming through now than we did a few years ago. We have constraints on fuel and, to some extent, on spares. They have given us some problems earlier this year, but on the whole we are now back on line with our training programme. We have something of a backlog of helicopter pilots, resulting from a period when ARGUS was out of action, both in the Adriatic and, more recently, during refit. That will take a bit of time to recover from. On the whole, we are now back on a firm and sustainable training programme.

Chairman

409. Just before we go on, there is one particular point here quoted from *Flight Deck*, where it says "The impact on "Sea King" training is being compounded by a shortfall in the number of submarines being made available for anti-submarine-warfare training". Is that a continuing problem?

(*Rear Admiral England*) It is not one I was aware of, Chairman. I cannot comment, but I can certainly come back to you on that, if you wish.

Chairman: I think if we could have a note on that it would be useful.

Mr Colvin

410. We have barter arrangements with the Germans and the Dutch. Presumably at least they have got enough submarines.

(*Rear Admiral Blackham*) We have submarines around the world. There are many chance or planned encounters of submarines in all parts of the globe. As a matter of interest (and I am sorry to keep quoting ARK ROYAL but it is about the only thing I know anything about!), the period in the Adriatic produced more submarine training time than I have had in the rest of my career, because the Mediterranean area had a number of submarines and we were able to make ad hoc arrangements to use them. We had a considerable amount of ASW training, both for ships and helicopters.

Chairman

411. Is that the first time an Admiral has had adequate training with regard to submarines?

(*Rear Admiral Blackham*) I have always been more than adequately trained, Chairman!

Mr Colvin

412. ARGUS's refit, and the fact that she was deployed in the Adriatic, has been quoted as a constraint. ARGUS was specially designed for operational flying training, so, presumably, while she has been unavailable you have been using RFA tankers and other vessels for this. Have they proved satisfactory?

(*Rear Admiral England*) Primarily we have used the Fort class, which are not obviously as adequate as ARGUS, as she is a purpose-built ship. We also use O class RFAs, the Olmeda type. Neither of those ships are, obviously, as ideal as ARGUS and they do not have the capacity—which is the major problem—of the number of helicopters that can be operated from that ship at the same time. So what tends to happen is that we have a backlog of pilot training to undertake once we get the full facility of ARGUS back—which is the situation we are in at the moment.

413. Has it been a serious constraint? In other words, do we really need a ship like the ARGUS, or could we do without her?

(*Rear Admiral England*) No. We have a backlog at the moment of about 18 months' work on helicopter—particularly Sea King—operational personnel training to get through. We can sustain that for a certain length of time by husbanding our already trained resources but that means deploying them in a way which is not conducive to their careers or to efficiency for the various individuals. So it is not something we can do without.

414. You have already referred to the Flight International article of 10 November and the shortage of submarines, but that article also refers to the question of Sea King availability, particularly in the two training squadrons, 810 at Culdrose and 706. I wondered if you would comment on those, because it was suggested that spares shortage is a serious problem.

(*Rear Admiral England*) Not perhaps entirely due to spares shortages. We have had difficulties with the availability of Sea Kings which has impinged, to some extent, on training and, marginally, on operational capability. It is a two-fold problem: one is that there has

[2]No cash changes hands; but the Portland Credit Scheme is in fact reflected in the appropriation account. A note on the Scheme is being prepared for the Committee and will cover this point.

[Mr Colvin *Cont*]

been in some specific areas—the rotary areas—some spares shortages consequent upon changes made in the procurement programme several years ago. These things take quite a long time to work through and it tends to be rather difficult to get them precisely right because you run things down because you have too many only to find two years later you have too few. We have made adjustments in that area, and the spares support for, particularly, Sea Kings, is just about adequate, but it has unfortunately come at a time when we had a major modification programme going on with Sea Kings, and indeed a lot of them are getting quite old in the tooth, so they are requiring more upkeep. So we have been on a knife-edge but we think we have got it under control now.

415. When you mentioned "a few years ago" you were referring to the moratorium of 1990/91?

(Rear Admiral England) No, I am talking more of the change in stores and cutbacks in 1992 which are now feeding through to us.

416. Tell us, how has the year in the Adriatic affected Sea Harrier training?

(Rear Admiral England) It has had no impact, as far as I am aware, on Sea Harrier training, but, again, I might turn to the expert from ARK ROYAL.

(Rear Admiral Blackham) I am not sure that I can comment. Operational training, of course, is first-rate, but if you are talking about pipeline training I am not, I am afraid, in a position to know whether that has reduced the number of aircraft available at Yeovilton.

(Rear Admiral England) As far as I am aware, there is no difficulty in supplying both pilots and aircraft.

Mr George

417. Before our Committee was set up in 1979 for the purposes of making life as difficult as possible for MoD, we had a predecessor Committee called The Defence and External Affairs Sub-Committee of the Expenditure Committee. That committee produced a report on tri-service training. The National Audit Office produced another report in 1987 on tri-service training. I would like to ask what progress has been made within the Royal Navy towards encouraging tri-service training.

(Rear Admiral Wilkinson) Perhaps I could start by just running through some of the training that is tri-service, or bi-service in some cases. On staff training, for example, we train together with the other two services at the Royal College of Defence Studies, the Joint Services Defence College and the Army's Higher Command and Staff College at Camberley. On the flying training side we do a fair amount with the Royal Air Force: elementary flying training, with fixed-wing basic training and advanced flying training and multi-engine flying training. We use the Joint School of Photography and the Joint School of Photographic Interpretation. Our air traffic controllers train with the Royal Air Force's; we do management training, information technology training and language training with the other services. Our Royal Marine drivers train with the Army; explosives, ordnance and demolition training we do with the Army, and we are just setting up now a joint diving school with the Army. We do, as

I mentioned earlier, a fair amount of second degree training at Shrivenham. So there is quite a lot that goes on already. Within the Ministry of Defence there is a committee called the Defence Training Committee, and one of its roles is to try and get the three services to exchange information on training, and where it is cost-effective we manage to do that training together. Sometimes there is a greater synergy not with the particular trade training in other services but with the other training which needs to be done in your own service. I think cooks' training is a good example of that. In the early 1980s the Naval Cookery School (and, indeed, the Air Force Cookery School) moved to St Omer Barracks in Aldershot where there was spare capacity, and we did training in the same location for some years. However, it was not the most cost-effective way of doing it, as we found to our experience. For a start we needed to have a naval administration cell there, which costs money which would not have been the case if it had been in a naval establishment. We found there was a higher training wastage amongst our young cooks because they were removed from the naval environment and everything that went with it, and the cooks still had to go back to a naval environment to do all the other things which were all part of a cook's training—ship's fire-fighting, decontamination, damage control, first aid, seamanship. So the sums eventually showed us this was not, as I say, the most cost-effective way of doing it. Last year the Army decided that St Omer Barracks no longer met the Food & Safety Act standards, and therefore they would have to change the way things were done. The investment appraisal which we then did showed it was actually more cost-effective to move the RN element back to the rest of the RN Supply School, HMS RALEIGH, than it was to continue with the Army. This is now happening. By doing this we shall not only get the synergy with the other naval training but also savings in administration by not being separate from the naval establishments.

418. If you cannot train cooks effectively, what chance have you got of training engineers effectively?

(Rear Admiral Wilkinson) Once again, one has to look at what appears from the point of the cost-effectiveness. We looked, two years ago, at air engineer training being done with the Air Force but found, again, that the Air Force's requirements for training were somewhat different from ours. This is because of the operational environment in which we and they work. If they have a serious aircraft problem they can back-load it to a third or fourth line depot where there are deep specialists to repair it; we have to carry out those repairs on board our ships. Therefore we require to train maintenance people to a deeper training and fewer specialists than the Air Force does. Even so, there are many common things between air engineering training in the Navy and Air Force. Again, however, we found the synergy with naval administration was the overriding factor, and cheaper to move HMS DAEDALUS to HMS SULTAN and share workshops there than it was to move them to a totally non-naval area, quite apart from the differences in the training I have mentioned.

419. I understand the facilities in Aldershot are pretty awful, and you said that they did not meet some

THE DEFENCE COMMITTEE 27

8 December 1993]	MR J MICHAEL MOSS, REAR ADMIRAL NICHOLAS J WILKINSON,	[Continued
REAR ADMIRAL JEREMY J BLACKHAM AND REAR ADMIRAL TIMOTHY J ENGLAND

[**Mr George** *Cont*]

public health standards. Could not the £2.2 million contract for a cookery school at RALEIGH have been spent on improving the facilities in Aldershot? Surely the palates of sailors are not completely different from those of airmen? It seems to me, as a surprisingly non-specialist in these matters, that the basic things could have been actually taught collectively, and then more specialist aspects back in-house, but the basic teaching could have been done on a tri-service basis, could it not?

(Rear Admiral Wilkinson) Yes, it is just that, as I understand it, it was a more expensive way of doing it. It is often more expensive to train collectively. This was the case when we actually weighed up the costs of having naval administration at Aldershot and moving people to and fro, with the very small number of people and ancillary instructors we shall have in HMS RALEIGH doing both instruction and administration.

420. When you look through your reply on the reasons why it was more sensible to "navalise" cooking, some of those arguments could actually be used as to why training should not be done at Southampton as opposed to Manadon. There seems to be quite a parallel with the arguments which had been used for retaining Manadon.

(Rear Admiral Wilkinson) Manadon is a whole establishment. What we are talking about here is moving one small part of one establishment into another establishment, so the comparison is not entirely valid. Southampton is not too far from other parts of the naval administration, and Southampton University will be supported in part by the existing naval infrastructure in the Portsmouth area.

Mr George: Thank you.

Chairman

421. Can we have a quick look at the simulators. When we went down to Portsmouth we saw the excellent Type 23 system in action, but we were concerned that the simulator of the Type 23 command system was not at that stage certain, or at least the date was not certain. We have now heard that that is going to come in in September 1998, but of course the first frigate equipped with the new system is going to have it by, I think, next year—that is, HMS WESTMINSTER—if indeed she has not got it already, so there is going to be a four-year gap between the system being operational and having a simulator to try it out, as it were, and to train it. Why was the simulator not ordered at the same time as the system, or why were the two not put together into the same timeframe?

(Rear Admiral Blackham) I think, Chairman, the Committee is well aware of the Type 23 command system saga, and you will be aware that it has taken some while to sort out precisely what that command system should be in the ships. Also, of course, it was not possible to design a training simulator until we knew what that system would be. So there is inevitably a time lapse between the finalisation of design of any system and subsequent pieces of work such as a training simulator. That is bound to follow on subsequently, and I do not think any of us is particularly happy about the early years of this saga. To a degree, we are in a recovery process. It would be a

mistake, I think, to assume that we cannot train people for the Type 23. As you have seen, there are various individual trainer simulators, and we are now subsequently putting together systems to pull this together and provide the proper command team training, but the fundamental problem lies in the early history of this saga.

422. It seems a very long time lapse.
(Rear Admiral Blackham) They are very complicated pieces of equipment.

423. Were the funds laid aside for a simulator to be ordered, or was this something also done subsequently?
(Rear Admiral Blackham) There are funds for a simulator to be ordered.

424. When were they allocated?
(Rear Admiral Blackham) I am not sure I am in a position to know that.

425. If somebody can discover, perhaps they can let me have a note.
(Mr Moss) You mean when in the past the provision was made, or when the provision falls now?

426. I presume the provision will now fall in 1998 when the thing is delivered.
(Mr Moss) We have covered the time in the note we have provided, Chairman, for the timing of the provision. That is now in progress.

427. What I wanted to know was the timing of when the original allocation was made; in other words, at what stage was it decided that it should be provided?
(Mr Moss) We shall let you know.
(Rear Admiral Blackham) It is the case that in the past trainers have not always been part of the project. That is no longer the case, and this is perhaps one of the happier consequences of this particular saga.

428. So on which side of that equation does this one fall?
(Rear Admiral Blackham) In the middle.

429. There is a black hole in the middle, I suspect. Can we then turn finally to market testing in the training area. I think I am right in saying that simulator maintenance and operation at HERON, OSPREY and SEAHAWK is to be, or has been, market tested, is that correct?
(Rear Admiral Blackham) We have got a comprehensive programme of doing feasibility studies in almost all of our training establishments to see which bits might lend themselves to either market testing or contractorisation, and whether we then proceed will depend on the outcome of those feasibility studies. You will appreciate that there are both financial and non-financial factors to be taken into account here, so we would in due course be examining the feasibility of almost all our training establishments and then proceeding on the outcome of those studies.

430. You have not actually answered the question, which is whether those three are already being market tested. However, perhaps that is not a fair question at this stage?
(Rear Admiral Blackham) Yes, it is for Fleet.

[**Chairman** *Cont*]

(*Rear Admiral England*) You mentioned specific simulators there.

431. Yes, HERON, OSPREY and SEAHAWK.

(*Rear Admiral England*) They are all establishments. I am a little confused. The answer is that the totality of the simulators which are used within FONA (Flag Officer Naval Aviation) are being looked at to decide which would be suitable to be run by a commercial operation and which are best suited to being run within the RN. There are other areas of FONA's activities in terms of pilot and observer training which are also being looked at in the same way.

432. How long is this feasibility study going to last?

(*Rear Admiral England*) It is due to report, I think, by the end of this year. It may even already be being considered. It is imminent.

433. When did it start?

(*Rear Admiral England*) At the beginning of this year.

Chairman: I do not think I have any further questions at this stage.

Mr Colvin

434. I have one question which may be not within the scope of this inquiry. We have been talking about training for service, but what about training for redundancy? There is a rundown in personnel, and there are a number of people facing compulsory redundancy in the Royal Navy. Is part of your brief to review and, if necessary, modify and expand the demob courses available to Royal Navy personnel?

(*Mr Moss*) We have a tri-service scheme in operation which is paying particular attention to the problem presented by redundancy and going, as it were, to great lengths to market the emerging serviceman to industry, stressing the great qualities of training and so on which he brings. Admiral Wilkinson may want to add to that.

(*Rear Admiral Wilkinson*) Of course, we do not train people specifically for civilian life. What we are trying to do is to improve the way in which service skills are related to civilian skills. The NVQ system is something of great interest to us. We have put a fair amount of effort into that in various different trade areas to help people leaving the service describe what they are able to do, and their experience, to civilian employers.

435. Are there any constraints placed upon you, as far as budget is concerned, for this purpose? Presumably, if there is more effort going into it, greater resources will be needed. Perhaps also you could say whether anything is being done about the spouses of Royal Naval personnel, because there are many instances where service personnel's wives or husbands are also employed either directly or indirectly by the services, and it is equally important to ensure that the husbands and wives are prepared for civilian employment when perhaps they have been dependent during their service on second incomes.

(*Rear Admiral Blackham*) I think there are very many fewer of those in the Navy than there are in the Army, by virtue of the nature of our business. Certainly within our own area in Portsmouth the number is very small. However, I am aware of the fear which you describe, and I am in discussion about it at the moment.

436. Is there any scheme by which you are sending redundant personnel for training?

(*Rear Admiral Blackham*) We run a system of——

437. The tri-service scheme?

(*Rear Admiral Blackham*) Yes. That is a system of resettlement courses, which you are probably aware of, in which people can obtain specific qualifications for specific areas. That system has been run for many years and is well used.

(*Rear Admiral England*) The resources devoted to it have indeed been increased recently because of the additional numbers.

Chairman: Thank you. I think that Bruce George would like to have one final crack.

Mr George

438. "Crack" is the right word, actually, Chairman! In the light of watching television recently, in which the Navy came out, I think, more or less ahead, is there any proposal to increase the training of sniffer dogs for the detection of drugs on board HM ships?

(*Rear Admiral Blackham*) There is plenty of evidence that they are doing very well already.

439. Is there tri-service training of sniffer dogs, or are they different dogs?

(*Rear Admiral England*) No, we have sea dogs in the Navy![3]

(*Mr Moss*) Could I come back to Mr George, seriously, on his very proper concern about tri-service training. I do want to assure him that of course the Department does have in mind the point which he makes to us, but the move which we discussed—the cooks from Aldershot—does depend on the facts of the case. We do not start with a clean sheet of paper where the answer might be different; we start with where we are now, and we do measure the costs of tri-service training or going the route of the single service, certainly.

440. I am sorry, I am not arguing a Canadian solution to our single service histories, but obviously where there is an improvement in the facility, yes, I would argue for tri-service training.

(*Mr Moss*) And we look at it, I do assure you, but sometimes the facts do take us in another direction.

Mr George: Absolutely. I totally support you on that.

Chairman: Thank you very much, Mr Moss, and thank you, gentlemen.

---

[3] The Royal Navy has four search dogs: all were trained at the Joint Service Dog Training Wing at Royal Air Force Newton.

WEDNESDAY 23 MARCH 1994[1]

Members present:

Sir Nicholas Bonsor, in the Chair

Mr Menzies Campbell   Sir Nicholas Fairbairn
Mr Churchill   Mr John Home Robertson
Mr Michael Colvin   Mr Peter Viggers
Mr Frank Cook

Examination of Witnesses

AIR VICE MARSHAL A J C BAGNALL OBE, Assistant Chief of the Air Staff, AIR VICE MARSHAL C C C COVILLE, Air Officer Training and MR JOHN R G CLARK, Head of Secretariat (Air Staff), Ministry of Defence, examined.

Chairman

1321. Good morning. Can you introduce your team please?

(*Air Vice Marshal Bagnall*) Thank you. May I start by introducing Air Vice Marshal Coville, who is the Air Officer Training from Support Command who is sitting on my right. On my left is Mr John Clark who is the Head of the Air Staff Secretariat in main building.

1322. Thank you very much. We are looking this morning at training and at low flying. What I propose to do is to take the first hour on training and then we will move on to low flying to make sure both sides get a fair hearing.

(*Air Vice Marshal Bagnall*) Thank you.

1323. First of all, can we look at the cut backs in the Royal Air Force in terms of pilots and aeroplanes. How easy would it be for you to reconstitute if we need to rebuild in a hurry?

(*Air Vice Marshal Bagnall*) Thank you for that because I recall that when we last met in this forum we talked about reconstitution and regeneration. I am in no doubt that the training machine, our ability to recruit young men and women and to bring them up to the ability to go to war is of crucial importance in this. In the work that has been done in Support Command and by my Air Force Board of Colleagues to make sensible savings in the training machine, we have had in mind the need to ensure that we have got sufficient airfields, that we have got sufficient infrastructure and sufficient trained people, ie the trainers themselves, such that if things do go wrong in the world and we have to start to build up again we can do so. It is not just the air crew where it takes some two to three years but as I think we mentioned before the senior NCO, the radar technician, the chap who has got the skills across the board, it can take seven or eight years to actually breed someone of that calibre, that skill level across the board. So we have taken great care to make sure that we have the ability to reconstitute should the need arise.

1324. As you say it would in fact take two to three years to train up an air crew under normal circumstances.

(*Air Vice Marshal Bagnall*) Under normal circumstances.

1325. How quickly would you be able to do that if there was a real emergency?

(*Air Vice Marshal Bagnall*) I think the difficulty is one does not really know what we are talking about because the crystal ball is cloudy as we again discussed beforehand. We have the ability at the moment to take people from the flying instructional posts, from the desk appointments, to use them to give us a surge capacity, to take them from the operational conversion units to augment the front line. We can do that very quickly. If you are going beyond that—and this is the area where we are talking about sustaining a commitment, endurance as the phrase is now used— you are then looking at the reserve force legislation, whether we can call up the recently retired people who are now either pensioners or doing a job in industry or whether we can resort to exceptional measures such as contracting training overseas. For instance, would we ask our fellow NATO countries, particularly America and Canada, to take some of the training tasks for us if it was purely a European commitment which is, again, a hypothetical situation. We are very much aware of the need to keep all the options open. On an item of detail, Sir Nicholas, we are looking at the moment at sending some multi-engined students to Canada to get first hand experience of their multi-engined training programme to make sure that we have a better understanding and also we send students at the moment on the Euro-NATO jet pilot training course in the States. So we do have some understanding of what is available to allow us to react at short notice.

Chairman: While we are on that subject, Sir Nicholas Fairbairn has something to ask.

Sir Nicholas Fairbairn

1326. I would have thought that if the news is to be believed Korea might be a slight problem shortly. At what notice could you have these people on standby?

(*Air Vice Marshal Bagnall*) Well I hope that Korea does not become a problem.

1327. It is a problem.

(*Air Vice Marshal Bagnall*) Well indeed it is a problem at the moment but it is not a problem, I hope, that will involve the European nations. I hope it will be contained by diplomacy. I hope that the measures that the American President appears to be taking will ensure that it does not grow from what appears to be a period of very significant tension at the moment to something beyond that.

Chairman: Sir Nicholas, we are talking about training, I do not really want to get into Korea, we are very short of time. Winston Churchill?

[1] The remainder of these Minutes of Evidence is published as HC314, Session 1993–94.

Mr Churchill

1328. How far and how vigorously was the possibility explored by the Royal Air Force and indeed by the Ministry of Defence and the Ministers of rather than cutting back in such a significant way, as is now being proposed, that we offer our facilities to certain selected allies given our, dare I say it, pre-eminence in this field? Was there such an approach made?

(*Air Vice Marshal Bagnall*) I will turn to my colleague in a moment, if I may, Mr Churchill, but to answer your question, what we have tried to do is to tailor the training machine that remains in the United Kingdom, a flying training machine, to meet our national requirements plus an element of headroom to cater for the unexpected. The difficulty is that we have some very successful multi-national training ventures—the Tornado establishment is a very good example—but the difficulty is that if we were to import training then it adds to noise, it adds to the burden of low flying and so on and so forth. I think the difficulty also is whether we would sustain a training machine in peacetime that was larger than we nationally needed for these sort of reasons having taken proper account of the need to expand should we have so to do.

1329. You have already said that it takes up to seven years to train somebody up to that sort of level, given that and the fact that you will never again have that sort of lead time or even half that lead time in the event of any future conflict——

(*Air Vice Marshal Bagnall*) Yes?

1330. ——or even approach much to a conflict, would it not be preferable to at least explore the possibility of whether we could not have say a 10 or 20 per cent increment on top of what we require for our national requirement which would be available to friendly governments to train up their pilots because presumably, particularly some of the smaller ones, I am thinking of Oman and others and possibly even Saudi Arabia, they might well welcome the services we could offer?

(*Air Vice Marshal Bagnall*) I think there are two points, if I may. The seven years related to the senior NCO, the technician, but even if we created the additional space you are talking about we would not be filling it with our own people and therefore we would still not necessarily have the chap with the seven years' experience because we do not need him to fill an established post at the moment. What we have done— and again you may recall I talked last time we met about the very significant cut back in recruiting that we have faced over the last year—we have reached exceptional arrangements with the Treasury such that we are recruiting—wrong word, sorry—we are making use of capacity by inviting some Kuwaiti students to come and actually fill it up so that we keep the bedrock training machine, the instructors, the buildings there so when we get to a steady state we have that infrastructure. I do not know, would you wish to add anything at this stage?

(*Air Vice Marshal Coville*) Well, Chairman, very little to add, other than to say that the Kuwaitis that ACAS referred to, we are actually getting 30 over the next two years during a period of downturn. I think we are becoming more dynamic in this area than perhaps we had been hitherto. Traditionally we have only taken five Foreign and Commonwealth training people, when I become a Chief Executive of the Training Group of Defence from 1 April onwards we will see far more flexibility in our costing criteria. We do expect to be able to exploit more any spare capacity we have in the training system without actually generating any spare capacity specifically for the task.

Mr Campbell

1331. Could I ask a question or two about instructors. What is the typical career profile of someone who finishes up as an instructor say on fast jets? Are these people who have had very considerable frontline experience, as it were, and who have been selected to become instructors because they are extremely good pilots or are they selected for that purpose because they appear to have the capacity to impart knowledge? How do you pick instructors and what sort of people are they?

(*Air Vice Marshal Coville*) If I can cover the initial instructors, those who teach in the training organisation, which is my responsibility, which takes people up to wings standard; there is a board which sits every year and very carefully people are scrutinised to check their suitability for instructional duties. We try to get a cross-section of people not just from one specific area largely because the instructor is very much a role model and it is very important as we stream during our training process to have a good cross-section of people with different backgrounds. So yes, there is a very close scrutiny being used to check their suitability before they come into the training organisation. Further downstream, after basic flying training they are largely people with an appropriate role background, so that those who instruct at the multi-engine advanced flying school, for example, are invariably people who have a credible background in a multi-engine large aeroplane. Equally, at the advanced tactical training unit, on the other hand, we again have people with a tactical or air defence background appropriate to the level at which they train.

1332. Is there any shortage of applicants for this, because it seems to me there are two fundamentals: the quality of the aircraft—and we hope we have secured that if we get the Eurofighter 2000—and there is the quality of the instruction. How do you ensure that you have maintained that quality?

(*Air Vice Marshal Bagnall*) There are two elements. There is the first that my colleague has spoken about, which is essentially taking people from the day they arrive in the Royal Air Force until they gain their wings standard. They then go forward to the operational conversion unit, where they are taught to fly and, if appropriate, to fight the aircraft that they will be using, for example Phantom** or Tornado. On the OCU there will be a mix of pure flying instructors, handling instructors and weapons instructors, who look at weapons/target matching, how to make sure the sight picture is correct, all these sorts of things. Once they leave the OCU they then go on to their first squadron, where they start to hone and develop these skills. On their first squadron there will be, in addition to the

---

² The Phantom has now been withdrawn from RAF Service.

[Mr Campbell *Cont*]

squadron commander and flight commander (who by necessity will be experienced), a specialist qualified flying instructor current on that type of aircraft, who can deal with the nuances of flying the Phantom* or the Tornado F3, who will do the annual evaluation, the instrument rating test and so on. In addition, there will be a weapons instructor, possibly two if it is a two-seater aircraft, a pilot and a navigator, to develop the more advanced skills, flying the aircraft to the edge of its safe manoeuvre limit, to make sure that the levels of excellence which I think you may have seen during your visit to Gioia del Colle and elsewhere are actually built into our crews over a number of years, so we split into a number of phases, the basic to get them flying, to get them comfortable in the air, and then to teach them either to fight that aircraft or, if it is a transport aircraft, to make sure they can operate it effectively and safely.

1333. Is there any shortage of people wanting to fulfil these specialist instructional roles?

(*Air Vice Marshal Bagnall*) No. We get a good cross-section and they come forward and they are jolly good people.

Chairman

1334. I will not ask you to go into it now but could you give us a list of the numbers of various instructors you have for the different roles?

(*Air Vice Marshal Bagnall*) Of course.

1335. Can we have a look at the Air Warfare Centre. I believe that is, as it were, a mobile group rather than a place, is that right, a group of people put together for this purpose?

(*Air Vice Marshal Bagnall*) Perhaps if I can touch a little bit on the background I can better answer your question. One of the key lessons out of the Gulf War was that when we faced an unexpected crisis we had the expertise, we had the people who could do the weapons to target matching, we had the people who could do the bomb damage analysis, we had the people who could look at the electronic warfare requirements and so on, but they were fragmented around the Air Force. One of the key lessons was that if we were to deal with the unexpected at short notice we needed to develop a centre of excellence which would allow the commander of the day to get at very short notice advice on the strategic planning for a campaign: do you go against the power station, do you go against the railways, do you go against the tanks that are deployed, the sort of mind-clearing, the grand strategy, but more important, or equally important, beneath that to look at how you would prosecute the campaign: do you need to take a bridge down with one large bomb or do you take two smaller bombs because a large bomb simply punctures a hole in it without exploding. What we have done is we have identified a number of expertises, the central trials and tactics organisation, people from our research branch, and we have moved them. We are forming a centre of excellence which will be based at Waddington and there are links to the Department of Air Warfare at Cranwell and to our Staff College at Bracknell and so on, and we are now building this up, so that in time we will have under a one-star lead a

³ibid.

centre of excellence. I have to say that I understand my Royal Navy colleagues are now looking to something similar to the work we are taking forward and there has been significant interest in this from my French and German colleagues also.

1336. Who is actually commanding that at the moment?

(*Air Vice Marshal Bagnall*) Air Commodore Lumsden is commanding it.

1337. Is that linked into your training schedules because I think that under the American pattern, which I think we are following, they have adopted training under one heading?

(*Air Vice Marshal Bagnall*) Yes. There is a training function but it is at the higher levels that I was speaking about earlier. For instance, the commandant of the air warfare centre runs the tactical leadership programme for the United Kingdom. There is a NATO tactical leadership programme. We are now running complementary courses, tactical leadership training courses, where we bring in, say, three or four Tornado F3 air defence aircraft, perhaps an E3 DF and perhaps a French E3, some tankers, and we mount large-scale raids against simulated targets, at sea or in the North of Scotland or wherever, to make sure we can respond at short notice, and we are stimulating the thought process that is so important to make sure that the youngsters are thinking forward, they are developing tactics against this very uncertain world that Sir Nicholas spoke about earlier.

1338. Can we then look specifically at personnel and training and personnel and training command, which is becoming an agency in ten days and Air Vice Marshal Coville is going to head it?

(*Air Vice Marshal Coville*) Yes. In fact, it is the training element of it rather than the whole command which will become an agency from 1 April.

1339. When that happens will there be a clearer breakdown of costs?

(*Air Vice Marshal Coville*) Yes. At the moment we are already embarking on refining our financial and management programmes and we have already made enough headway on producing a proper asset register, which we have lacked in the past. We are also incorporating over the next two years a financial and management accounting system which will enable us to work to a proper full cost accrual based process, which will be far more credible as far as our accounts are concerned in the future and it will be far easier for me, as Chief Executive, to define costs.

1340. At the moment I suppose it is too early for you to say whether you reckon your costs and resources are going to match adequately?

(*Air Vice Marshal Bagnall*) Perhaps I could take that because one of my responsibilities is to offer advice to my Standing Committee colleagues on the Air Force programme at large and we are only too conscious that we have to drive down costs as best we sensibly can to ensure that we keep the teeth end of the Air Force in good shape. There has been a lot of very lateral thinking, a lot of very useful initiatives already taken

[**Chairman** *Cont*]
forward by AOCinC Support Command and AOT and others to look at the training machine, to make the best use of contractor support, where it is appropriate, for servicing. So to answer your question, yes, that is at the forefront of our minds at the moment.

1341. The Agency has been quite a long time in gestation (if I can put it that way) because our predecessor Committee was told in 1991 that "the Training Group's relationship to, and division of responsibilities with, the RAF Headquarters elements concerned with Training policy and practice" had given rise to some difficulties. That, I presume, has now been ironed out?
(*Air Vice Marshal Coville*) Yes. One of the main difficulties was the responsibility that was held in London for forward policy, which to some extent did clash with the responsibility of the Chief Executive. As part of the Prospect re-organisation, my responsibilities also now embrace this policy, so that has removed one of the major hurdles to agency status.
(*Air Vice Marshal Bagnall*) There was also a cost to it, to set it up, and at the same time we were forming other agencies. It was simply a question of pressure, resources and allocation but, as I think you have been told, we are now poised to go into agency status and are very optimistic about it.

1342. If I can put in a slightly mischievous question, given the cost of the refurbishment of the four-star air officer commander in chief of personnel and training's house, can I take it that Air Vice Marshal Coville's house is not going to be similarly treated?
(*Air Vice Marshal Bagnall*) Air Marshal Coville will describe his house to you. I have not had the pleasure of visiting it but I am told it is a very modest new house built by a large corporation such as Wimpey or Barratt.

1343. It will be very difficult to spend that much money on a house like that, I suspect.
(*Air Vice Marshal Coville*) For the record, Chairman, my house was built as part of the small new estate houses constructed as part of the re-organisation and Mowlem actually were the contractors.

Mr Churchill
1344. Chairman, can I, just to put that matter in context, say that it was reported within the last ten days that an individual with a large family who happens to be unemployed had over £100,000 spent on his home by the local authority, and that was not an air marshal.
(*Air Vice Marshal Bagnall*) I am very grateful for that clarification.

Chairman
1345. That will be noted. Coming back to slightly more serious matters, the recent changes at Cranwell, I believe the balance between graduate and non-graduate entry has changed. Can you say a word or two about that and what effects the review of command and staff training at Bracknell might have had?
(*Air Vice Marshal Coville*) There has been no substantial difference in our long-term plot between the graduate and non-graduate entries. At the moment we have, as you are aware, a very reduced intake. The

large majority of people who go to Cranwell this year and next will be those to whom we already have a commitment. That is largely the university cadetships and the bursars. The substantial change that we have made at Cranwell over the last years has been an increase from 18 to 24 weeks in our initial officer training. It is more than just a chronological change, we have actually changed the emphasis and we believe we have a far better course as a result.

1346. And at Bracknell?
(*Air Vice Marshal Coville*) As far as the implications of the entry standard are concerned, we see no significance of that to Bracknell. As you are aware Command and staff training is being reviewed under the defence cost study.

1347. That is really what I was getting at.
(*Air Vice Marshal Bagnall*) Yes. It is one of the range, Sir Nicholas, and the reports will come forward in due course.

1348. Is there any reason why both Cranwell and Bracknell should not be part of the training agency under your command? Is it really necessary to have two more two-star commanders in chief?
(*Air Vice Marshal Coville*) We have looked at this in the past. Both Bracknell and Cranwell have a very discrete responsibility. Both are run by two stars and they have their own management plan and their own clearly defined budget. The studies that we have instigated in the past have made it absolutely clear that there is no overlap between my responsibility and those of the other two two-stars. Again, however, this whole business is being looked at under the defence cost study.

1349. No doubt we will see what may come out of it. Finally, under this heading, if I can turn to catering, for a moment. The Navy, as you know, have pulled out of the Aldershot Catering School and are going to retain people separately. The reason we were given by the naval commanders was that there was a different ethos from the army. It is understandable that cooking in the galley is rather different from cooking in the field. There was also the question of basic training which was different for the three services, at least I assume it was different for the three services even for the catering staff. Are you happy that the RAF can go on training at Aldershot with the army and does that give any particular difficulties and problems for your people?
(*Air Vice Marshal Coville*) There are, of course, differences in the equipment used by the three services and this is really the point of the Royal Navy's thrust to their argument. In fact, for slightly different reasons, we have decided that we will go back to one of our previous locations for our chef training and that is Royal Air Force Halton as part of the ground training rationalisation programme. The main reason for this is that the Sandamer Barracks, the large block that undertakes the tri-service training for the moment, is getting very close to the end of its useful life and a thorough investment appraisal showed quite clearly that the cheaper option was to absorb, in our case, Royal Air Force cookery training at Royal Air Force Halton which is part of our ground training future programme.

[Chairman *Cont*]

1350. So when will that move take place?

(*Air Vice Marshal Coville*) That will take place within a year.

Sir Nicholas Fairbairn

1351. Can I ask what you mean by "we use different equipment"? If you are boiling an egg you use a pan, if you are making spaghetti you use a pan, I cannot understand the difference in equipment.

(*Air Vice Marshal Coville*) It tends to be what is underneath the pan rather than the pan itself, Sir Nicholas. Obviously on board a ship the type of equipment which is appropriate to a galley on a ship is very different from that which is appropriate on a large Royal Air Force station and indeed on an army base.

Mr Campbell: This is low frying!

Mr Cook: Trust him to steal my jokes!

Mr Campbell: You have to be quick.

Chairman: I think we will move off the catering subject.

Mr Cook: Trying to keep the Cook quiet again you see.

Chairman: I will not follow that up with an even more appropriate pun. Peter Viggers would you take us on to individuals and their units?

Mr Viggers

1352. Turning to basic physical fitness, there is obviously a physical before personnel are accepted into the service. How often are physical fitness tests renewed and what happens if people do not meet them?

(*Air Vice Marshal Coville*) During early training, that is initial and basic and so on, there is on-going emphasis on physical fitness, getting people up to a standard appropriate to their future careers in the Royal Air Force. This is re-emphasised when people come back for further training courses later in their service careers. As far as annual fitness is concerned we have recently embarked on two programmes. One is a Healthy Heart Campaign, for want of a better expression, we have signed up for that over the last six months. There is an emphasis now very much on the whole man and woman being fit both in their diet and in their way of life. In addition to that from 1 January we have implemented an annual fitness test for all people under 50, over 50 it is voluntary. It is geared to the age of the person but everyone is required at or about their birth date to undertake a fitness test.

Mr Viggers: I am slightly surprised to hear the test is voluntary over the age of 50. I would have thought—as one who is over 50—it is important to be fit.

Chairman

1353. Some of us, on the other hand, might take a different view.

(*Air Vice Marshal Coville*) I think you have made your own point, Sir.

Mr Viggers

1354. Military skills: is there a basic training which involves drills and is this continued later? Are there basic personal weapons skills for all persons?

(*Air Vice Marshal Coville*) Yes. Later in a person's career everyone is required, on an annual basis, to renew his skill level. We have a new programme called the Common Core Skills—CCS—which examines very much the ability to carry weapons—NBC, first aid, basic military skills. In addition to that those people who are required to carry arms on live arm guarding duty every three months must undertake a two day refresher, particularly on safety checks' scenarios, that is a very closely controlled, closely co-ordinated check of their ability to carry out their live armed guard duty.

1355. Some personnel, like air crew obviously, have minimum standards they must comply with—minimum number of hours and so on—are you able to apply comparable standards across the whole of the Royal Air Force including the Supply and Secretariat area? Is there a test of technical proficiency you are able to impose?

(*Air Vice Marshal Bagnall*) Perhaps I could take that. If you are talking about war fighting skills as opposed to administrative skills then there are periodic reviews. We are seen to be at the forefront of the NATO tactical evaluation system. One difficulty we have had here is that in the old days it was clear cut, we were defending the main operating bases in the United Kingdom and we practised accordingly. Now one of the challenges is to create a scenario where we can replicate the sort of short notice deployment, possibly a bare base with little host nation support but we are developing these to make sure that not only our air crew but our ground crew, our senior NCOs, our logisticians and so on can continue to meet their operational functions in simulated NBC conditions and so on. There is a rigorous programme of not only developing the skills but evaluating them also. So I am confident that the arrangements we have in place are very robust in this respect.

1356. I understand what you said that you are developing a system of evaluation of fitness and readiness.

(*Air Vice Marshal Bagnall*) No, sorry, let me correct myself, what I am saying is we are trying to re-shape it to today's threat where the threat is not one of defending static bases in the United Kingdom against the Russian special forces or incoming fighter bomber raids. At the moment, it is more likely, unfortunately, that we will have to deploy overseas. We have got forces in Northern Iraq, Southern Iraq and Bosnia and who knows where we will be tomorrow? So what I want to try and do is to develop the leadership skills, the military skills, the professional skills so that we can go to either a bare base or a base where the host nation provides water, cooking and so on to make sure that we can quickly fit into that and get on and prosecute the job in hand.

1357. Turning specifically to the flying training and flying skills, how constrained do you feel in terms of live firings and bombings and can you give me examples of how many live Sidewinder firings will a Tornado F3 be allowed during a year?

(*Air Vice Marshal Bagnall*) Yes. There are obvious constraints in that weapons cost money but we are fortunate in that we need to periodically make sure that weapons that are sitting on the shelf have not decayed, that there is no wiring falling down. We also need to

[Mr Viggers Cont]

give the air crews confidence that when they pull the trigger the weapons' system as a whole will work. Having said that we make great use of synthetic training because it is damn nigh impossible to replicate large scale raids with electronic warfare with enemy opposition in today's peacetime environment. But to answer your specific question, if I may just refer to the piece of paper here, air defence crews on average will fire one Skyflash and one Sidewinder per crew during their tour and the strike attack and offensive support crews, who are only equipped with the Sidewinder, will fire one missile every three to four years.

1358. And the Jaguar crews, the CVR 7?

(Air Vice Marshal Bagnall) The Jaguar crews will go on to the ranges three to four times a week. In terms of the particular weapons they will drop, normally they will drop practice weapons because there is a difficulty if we drop CBUs (cluster bomb units) with the bomblets in them; it can only be done on very selected ranges in case you get a bomblet that does not go off and you then have to clear it and so on. But what I can assure you—and again I hope those of you who went to Gioia del Colle saw this—is that our crews are optimistic and confident that the weapons on their aircraft will work and do work and they get sufficient practice in using them.

1359. Finally, do you feel a constraint in the use of fuel for flying training and are pilots getting all the flying experience you would like them to have, or do you feel there is a lack of it?

(Air Vice Marshal Bagnall) You are addressing the question to two slightly elderly pilots who trained together over the years. The answer to that is that a pilot by and large will always want to go and do more. He wants to increase the level of excellence, he wants to make the best use of the equipment he has. We have had over the years to take very careful decisions on the amount of flying that we do because it is not just the fuel, it is the engineering support that goes with it. Every sortie can lead to spares consumption, be it a brake parachute or a practice weapon. We are satisfied—indeed my Standing Committee colleagues discussed this at length some time ago and we are satisfied that the amount of flying that we provide for our crews is adequate for the requirements they are likely to face.

Mr Colvin

1360. Chairman, before we get off the subject of individuals and units, can I raise the question of reserves because the RAF reserves are not large. I think the RAF Volunteer Reserve is now down to about 180 men; it was 200?

(Air Vice Marshal Bagnall) That sort of figure. I am sorry, I have not got the detailed figures.

1361. But the Royal Auxiliary Air Force does have rather more men in it, some 2,000 or so, and a lot of those are specialists. What is being done to keep them technically up-to-date because some of them will be engaged on maritime patrols and electronic warfare, so there is a need for regular updates?

(Air Vice Marshal Bagnall) There are a number of elements to your question. One difficulty we have is that in the case of the reserve forces that the Royal Air Force had, several of them were tied to the defence of our main bases in the United Kingdom.

1362. RAF Regiment and units like that?

(Air Vice Marshal Bagnall) RAF Regiment, auxiliary field squadrons and so on. What we have had to do is to look at the changed operational environment, the need to have mobility, the lessons that came out of the Gulf War, to make sure the mix we have at the moment is about right. We are continuing now with a whole range of studies and it would be wrong for me to go into detail at this stage and we have yet to bring firm proposals to Ministers, but what I can assure you is that we have some innovative ideas and we are hoping to return shortly to some airborne flying for our reservists and one or two other areas and I hope that when we perhaps meet again we can discuss it in more detail. But to answer your question, we are looking across the board at how we can make better use of reservists that are available to us.

1363. And when a man or woman leaves the RAF do they automatically go on a reserve so that they could be called up?

(Air Vice Marshal Bagnall) Yes, they have a commitment for a number of years depending on their rank, their length of service and their particular specialisation. We track them, we keep a track on their location, we test the ability to get hold of them should we need to. So there are some 30-odd thousand retired personnel, pensioners and whatever that we could in a time of crisis call on.

1364. With the Army there is an obligation for regular reservists to do some training. I do not think many of them do but is that so with the RAF as well?

(Air Vice Marshal Bagnall) We also have the same requirement. The difficulty or the reality is that we have not enforced it in the past, in part because of the cost of so doing and in part because of the difficulty of tracking people when they leave and the mobility of society. What we have now established at our Personnel Management Centre at Innsworth is the ability to track these people, so this is one of the very areas we are looking at at the moment, as to the extent to which we call them back each year for periodic refresher training: is it a week, is it ten days, what is it going to cost and what are the trade-offs in terms of benefit, because one of the difficulties that we foresee is that by and large we are looking for high-tech people and these are the very people who are on the Eurofighter production line, working to a fixed-price contract to get it out on cost on time, and we are getting a sense that in some areas industry may be somewhat reticent to release them for the amount of training we would have in mind and this is an area we are looking at at the moment.

1365. Are you also looking at the idea of the sponsored reserve?

(Air Vice Marshal Bagnall) Yes, we are.

Mr Campbell

1366. What is the sanction if someone fails the physical fitness test?

(Air Vice Marshal Coville) He is first of all offered a remedial package.

[Mr Campbell *Cont*]

1367. What does that consist of?

(*Air Vice Marshal Coville*) That really is going back a little. I have to say that the physical fitness test is really only there to make sure that people can meet minimum physical requirements, so it is not looking for someone with the ability to move straight into the SAS. So far the success rate has been very good. Obviously it is early days but only a very few people so far have failed. Those people who have failed are offered a remedial package. Subsequently, if they continue to fail, their future careers will be re-examined.

1368. That has put it, if I may say so, rather generally. Perhaps I could put the question more bluntly and I might get a blunter answer. If people consistently fail may they be dismissed the service?

(*Air Vice Marshal Coville*) That, of course, has to be a possibility. As you know, there is a set procedure for those people who fail to achieve the standards required of them.

(*Air Vice Marshal Bagnall*) If I can add something, if it is a case of someone who is overweight, unfit, then it is in their own interests if they want to progress through the service to do something about it. We will offer them every encouragement that it is entirely likely that their career progression will be held back if they do not do something about it. If it is a stage beyond that, that someone is patently unfit because they are smoking dramatically heavily or for whatever other reason, then there are further steps that we can take against them. In the final analysis, if someone has a self-induced unfitness problem (if I can put it in those vague words) then they will be invited to leave the service.

1369. How high is the basic standard? I know you are not looking for people to go "yomping" across the Falklands at 12 hours' notice with 40lbs on their backs but what level of fitness are you looking for in the ordinary course?

(*Air Vice Marshal Bagnall*) We are looking for someone who, in terms of the aircrew, can fly four demanding sorties, keep going on a very modest amount of sleep and keep going on like that for as long as the war goes on. In terms of the groundcrew, we are looking for someone who can run across the pan, load a Sidewinder missile, go out on a dark and wet night and defend the perimeter. What we are not looking for is a man to yomp up the side of the Cairngorms at short notice. We are looking for someone who is fit to fight.

Sir Nicholas Fairbairn

1370. Do you still have the five-mile bash or was that never part of Air Force procedures?

(*Air Vice Marshal Bagnall*) It was part of the Cranwell system, Sir Nicholas. When I had the pleasure of going there many years ago, it was called the "knocker cup", but we do not have something quite the same these days.

Chairman

1371. What is the test, in fact? Is it a one-mile run, a ten-mile run?

(*Air Vice Marshal Bagnall*) I am sorry, I do not have the details to hand.

(*Air Vice Marshal Coville*) I think I can give you it in general terms. It is called a bleep test and in essence people run from one side of the gymnasium to the other. The time interval between the bleeps gets shorter until eventually it is quite obvious that someone has to stop. That is then checked against an appropriate set of standards, which takes into account age and so on. The person is then told whether he has passed or failed. Above the age of 40 that is replaced with a bicycle test. Perhaps some of your colleagues have themselves used an exercise bicycle. It is pretty well the same thing. The heart rate, blood pressure and so on are measured during the time someone is on the bicycle. There is also a grip test for most people over 40 to check that their limb strength is adequate for their primary task.

Chairman: I do not want to dwell on this too long.

Mr Cook: I do not either, Chairman. I just want to point out that if the assessors came to the House of Commons they would not get many people who would pass the test!

Mr Campbell: Speak for yourself!

Chairman

1372. I notice Mr George is absent from the Committee this morning. He must have known what we were going to talk about! Before we move on to the next topic, can I come back to the question of the constraints on training flying hours. How do we compare in our training flying hour schedule with our NATO allies?

(*Air Vice Marshal Bagnall*) We compare very favourably. Again if you would like a table showing the details I will be glad to provide that for you.

1373. Thank you, that would be extremely helpful. Have you actually had to cut back recently as a result of any financial constraints of any kind or the availability of spares on your training hour requirement?

(*Air Vice Marshal Bagnall*) No, when we went through the last LTC process, that is just about now put to bed, LTC 94, inevitably one of the questions was asked "Was the RAF flying too much/too little", and the judgment there was we had it about right and so there have been no recent adjustments made.

Chairman: Thank you. Moving on more specifically to flying training then I will ask Frank Cook to lead us on that subject.

Mr Cook

1374. Air Vice Marshal, what is your latest assessment of the progress being made on a major review of the flying training programme?

(*Air Vice Marshal Bagnall*) Perhaps my colleague could answer that.

(*Air Vice Marshal Coville*) We have been doing this for quite a long time, as you know, and it really started some two or three years ago with an examination of the equipment that we had. As a result of that we have replaced our basic flying training aircraft, the Jet Provost with a Tucano. That is coming into service very successfully. It is an extremely cheap aeroplane to run. It uses about a third of the fuel of the Jet Provost and the running costs are appropriately lower. We have also contractorised the elementary stage of flying training. This is where those people with little or no previous flying experience are given the motor skills appropriate

[**Mr Cook** *Cont*]

to bring them on the Tucano. In the past we used the Chipmunk, which again is an old aeroplane, rather expensive to run. That has now been given to a contractorised organisation at Topcliffe, Royal Air Force Topcliffe near to Linton in Yorkshire using the Firefly which many of us will know has recently been awarded the British Design Council award. Very nice aeroplane to fly and it is doing the job admirably. As far as our basing is concerned, the last two to three years we have been undergoing quite considerable rationalisation which started with the closure of Church Fenton and its reduction to a relief landing ground status. Shortly thereafter we closed one of our three Hawk bases and rationalised our Hawk flying training. Now we have what we call a mirror image Hawk flying training system which is conducted, for the time being, at Valley and at Royal Air Force Chivenor but you will be aware with the continuing fast jet throughput reduction it has been announced that we will be putting Chivenor on care and maintenance in the next year. In fact we cease flying training there in October of this year. We are continuing with our rationalisation studies. We hope to continue to reduce the size of our estate to make it appropriate to the task in future and we have no doubt we shall do so and maintain our traditionally high standard.

1375. Excellent reply, you have taken away half of my questions.
(*Air Vice Marshal Bagnall*) May I just add one point? The fact that we put Chivenor on to care and maintenance as opposed to closing the station reflects our concern about reconstitution and regeneration because it means that *in extremis* we could re-activate the station at very short notice because the infrastructure will remain.

1376. As I understood it, at Chivenor and Brawdy there was a kind of operational lead in training but you have merged that with the Advanced Flying Training at Valley?
(*Air Vice Marshal Coville*) Yes.

1377. But at the same time, as I understand it, there is a fall in the number of hours being flown. Has this had any effect on the outcome of capability?
(*Air Vice Marshal Coville*) The previous courses, the Advanced Flying Training School at Valley gave approximately 70 hours of in essence pure flying with some low level, tactical formation and so on, but the applied flying was done on a course of around 60 hours at one of the tactical weapons units either at Brawdy or at Chivenor. We found when we looked at this there was considerable overlap between what was done at the tail end of the Valley course and that which was done at the early stages of the Chivenor and Brawdy course. Also, inevitably, moving from one base to another, on relatively short courses, was in itself inefficient and moving to a new base requires confirmation of a chap's flying ability with new instructors and so on and so forth. The overall reduction has been from about 130 down to 100 hours. We have managed to retain all of the essential elements of both the Advanced Flying Training Schools and the Tactical Weapons Unit. We have actually managed to increase in one area Air to Air Gunnery which had previously been dropped and

we have re-introduced that to the 100 hour syllabus. One area where we have reduced a little is in the young man's practice leadership of the tactical formation. We believe that is appropriate to the changed world scene but we await, nevertheless, the comments from further downstream on the operational conversion units and we stand ready to adjust our courses if necessary to do so.

1378. You make it sound as though you are managing a lot better without the Tactical Weapons Unit?
(*Air Vice Marshal Coville*) Of course that role has been subsumed within the Valley and Chivenor courses. We are certainly not doing without it, we have just adjusted the course to absorb it on one base rather than on two.

Chairman

1379. Before we leave Chivenor, there have been strong rumours that the Marines Logistic Unit might move to Chivenor, is that something which would give the RAF problems?
(*Air Vice Marshal Bagnall*) I have not heard those rumours, Mr Chairman, until one knew the details, I could not comment.

Sir Nicholas Fairbairn

1380. Separate catering.
(*Air Vice Marshal Bagnall*) I am sorry, I do not know.

Chairman

1381. Will you see if there is any truth?
(*Air Vice Marshal Coville*) All I can tell you is that the Marines have visited and done an early reconnaissance but we have no further details on that.

Mr Cook

1382. Did they tell you that they were coming!
(*Air Vice Marshal Coville*) Yes, and I can assure Sir Nicholas Fairbairn that they were well fed.

1383. Can we turn specifically to the European Fighter 2000, what progress have you made in addressing the training tasks that are going to be necessary there? Obviously it is going to involve Operational Conversion Units.
(*Air Vice Marshal Bagnall*) There is a number of elements to your question. We are giving very significant thought to how we prepare for the Eurofighter. We are talking to the other nations about whether there is merit in having a multi-national training environment. The difficulty there is that the United Kingdom is seeking a truly multi-role aircraft that would deal with air defence, ground attack and recognisance whereas our partners at the moment are seeking to use it principally in the air defence roles so it may not be straight forward. There is also the question of where the facility would go because there will be a need, undoubtedly, for some low flying and the noise that will be associated with a large training establishment. So at the moment those discussions are at an early stage and it is impossible to predict which way they will go. In terms of synthetic training aids—

[Mr Cook *Cont]*

the simulator and the like—a lot of work is going on there building on the work that we did for the Harrier GR7 where we have a very sophisticated simulator at the moment at Wittering and indeed technologies that are available elsewhere around the world to make sure that we can get a simulator that best meets our need. In terms of the structure of the force, the basing, where the Operational Conversion Unit will go, the national training unit, those plans are still being developed at the moment, Mr Cook, and we are talking, as you know, some years downstream. What I can assure you is that all these items have been looked at, as indeed are the lead into Eurofighter, whether the 100 hours' course that Air Marshal Coville has spoken about is the sort of thing we want or whether we need to refine it nearer the time.

1384. Will the Tucano and the Hawk be adequate preparation?

(*Air Vice Marshal Bagnall*) We believe so. What we are going to give some thought to, and I have not yet set the work in hand, is whether we need to look at the Hawk in terms of the cockpit displays and the ability to put high workload situations on the crew, on the pilot in particular, whether they are appropriate to Eurofighter and that work is just about to be set in hand.

1385. If we can turn specifically to navigators and the training there: with the European Fighter Aircraft replacing Tornado F3s and other models too I guess and the 130J needing no navigator on what premise is the predicted 45 annual steady rate of training based from 1995 onwards?

(*Air Vice Marshal Coville*) Yes, the 45 strength of navigators has been determined by an assumption, no more than that at this stage, of the purchase of the J-model Hercules and then for the in-service on time. It has also taken into account the numbers and therefore the date of entry into service of the Eurofighter 2000. Of course, to some extent, as best as we possibly can at the moment, it does take into account some of the decisions we believe will arise from the defence cost study. That is, if you like, our best possible calculation with the assumptions that we make at the moment.

1386. That is subject to modification clearly.

(*Air Vice Marshal Coville*) Yes.

1387. Operational Conversion Units, will they be integrated with Tour Operational Units as with the Nimrod?

(*Air Vice Marshal Bagnall*) The Operational Conversion Unit is seen as being a necessary step for taking the young man who at this stage will have flown the Tucano and the Hawk to wean him on to the more advanced aircraft. The question really is whether they are integrated within the wing; in other words, whether the aircraft are held as an identifiable single unit, as is the case with the Tornado F3, or whether the aircraft form part of the larger wing, as is the case with the Charlie 130. The arrangements we have at the moment we are broadly satisfied give us the best value for money, give us the most sensible and expeditious route to get people to their combat ready status. However, this is one of the things that we are looking at at the moment as part of the Defence Cost Study to see whether there are any measures we can take here further to streamline the arrangements we have at the moment.

1388. When do you expect to finalise your considerations?

(*Air Vice Marshal Bagnall*) I would guess over the next two or three months.

Mr Cook: There are a number of other issues but I think we can deal with them in another way.

Chairman

1389. I think so, yes. Whilst on the OCUs still, can you give the Committee any idea of what the disadvantages might be of integration?

(*Air Vice Marshal Bagnall*) The difficulty is that if you have a unique OCU you have a pool of expertise and in a large force you have a centre of excellence where you send people to learn to fly, to learn to fight the aircraft, and then they go out to their units. The counter-argument is that if you disperse those aircraft you increase the size of the squadrons, you do more training on the squadrons, you reduce the overheads because you do not have this unique dedicated unit. The difficulty is that you then need also to put the training people that Mr Campbell was talking about earlier, the qualified flying instructors and the weapons instructors, out to the individual units and what you tend to lose is the centre of excellence where people come together, where they share ideas, where they meet their colleagues from other nations. In the final analysis one has to look at the costs and look at the overheads of the various structures, and I guess at the end of the day there is a subjective judgment on the premium you want to pay for degrees of excellence.

Chairman: Thank you very much. Can we turn to ground training and I will ask Winston Churchill to deal with that.

Mr Churchill

1390. Your November 1992 proposals, have they progressed as hoped and will there be market testing of teaching the technical trades?

(*Air Vice Marshal Coville*) Yes, the ground training rationalisation plan, the GTR 1, as we call it, has progressed very well indeed and all those things on which you have been briefed in the past will happen on time. As far as market testing is concerned, we do indeed intend to market test certain, what we call non-military aspects of ground training, and these will be put to the market as part of our market testing process now under way.

1391. So far as RAF Newton is concerned, why do you propose to keep an enclave there?

(*Air Vice Marshal Coville*) The reason for the enclave is that there are one or two areas which are in the short term difficult to move and are dependent upon further studies, for example, the future of the Defence Animal Centre, which is based at Melton Mowbray. The ground training rationalisation looked at moving ground training into more rational locations and that is what we are doing. Newton has a very large number of disparate units. Those units which are not specifically ground training were not subsumed within the ground

[Mr Churchill *Cont]*

training rationalisation study. Clearly their future is
being examined and one in particular, the future of the
Dog Centre, is now the subject of investment appraisal.

1392. As far as the ground communications training
is concerned at RAF Locking, will it now move to
Halton?

(*Air Vice Marshal Coville*) That is the subject of
study under ground training rationalisation part 2.
There is an investment appraisal which is at present
being studied.

1393. When will that be decided?

(*Air Vice Marshal Coville*) We hope to have the
paper to the Air Force Board some time this summer
and to ministers two to three months thereafter.

1394. You are foreseeing a "steady state" intake of
groundcrew of 5,750, even if only by the end of the
decade, but if (as Mr Portillo appears to want) you are
heavily civilianised, how far could you actually save on
ground training costs, or are they fixed to a large
degree?

(*Air Vice Marshal Bagnall*) Again we come back to
the reconstitution, regeneration point. What we have
tried to do is to develop a ground training structure that
will meet our forecast needs. If it transpires that the
throughput is less than that, for whatever reason—

either the requirement decreases or retention is better
than anticipated—it will create some headroom, as you
are suggesting. What we would seek to do then is to fill
that headroom, as we have done in the case of the flying
training machine, by inviting, for example, the
Kuwaitis to send some students along, but by and large
we are satisfied that by coming down to the sort of
structures we have we are at the minimum that we
would wish to go to with a view to being able to
reconstitute and regenerate.

Sir Nicholas Fairbairn

1395. Have you advised Mr Portillo by any chance
that somebody who is in the Services works as many
hours as is required for the same pay, whereas a
civilian does not, he requires overtime, and it is
actually infinitely more expensive to have civilians who
do not know what they are doing than it is to have
servicemen who do?

(*Air Vice Marshal Bagnall*) I regret I have not had
the chance to meet Mr Portillo recently, Sir Nicholas.

Sir Nicholas Fairbairn: Sir Nicholas and I met him
yesterday.

Chairman: I am sure Sir Nicholas, who I do not think
made that point yesterday, will take the earliest
opportunity to make it the next time he meets Mr
Portillo. That completes, I think, what we wanted to say
about training.

WRITTEN EVIDENCE

**Asterisks in the evidence denote that part or all of a question or answer thereto,
or a passage of evidence, has not been reported, at the request of the
Ministry of Defence and with the agreement of the Committee.**

1. **Memoranda submitted by the Ministry of Defence answering the Committee's questions
on Military training** (2, 6 and 8 July 1993)

Q1. It would be helpful to have an organisation chart for the Inspector General of Doctrine and Training, showing numbers, roles and responsibilities.

A1. The Inspector General of Doctrine and Training (IGDT) has four principal objectives:

— To provide the Ministry of Defence and Field Army with an authoritative land warfare doctrine which will enhance the fighting effectiveness of the Army.

— To advise MOD staffs on changes to the organisations and capabilities of land forces in pursuance of that doctrine.

— To formulate the Army's policy on individual and collective training.

— To ensure that the Army has the trained manpower that it requires to implement its doctrine by:

   (a) the provision of the required infrastructure to implement Army Training Policy.

   (b) Inspecting standards of individual training worldwide.

In pursuit of these objectives IGDT commands the Arms Directors and their training centres, Service training centres, the Officer Colleges, the Initial Training Group and certain Defence Training establishments.

STAFFING

To meet these objectives IGDT will, following co-location at Upavon in August of this year, be established with a staff of 103 military and 116 civilian personnel, and an organisational chart for the headquarters Doctrine and Training is attached at Annex A. In total, as at 1 April 1993, the Army Training Organisation employs 10,892 military and 7,177 civilian personnel, and is designed to deal with a throughput of 15,000 Phase I and II trainees.

FINANCE

IGDT is a Higher Level Budget holder in the CinC UKLF Top Level Budget, with a FY 93/94 allocation of £526 million. The budgetary structure which applies is shown at Annex B*.

Q2. It would be helpful to have available figures, showing results over recent years of tests of individual soldiers' skills, in particular the Annual Personal Weapons Test and Combat/Battle Fitness tests, indicating any recent changes in standards.

A2. At present Army Personnel Weapons Test results are only held at District/Brigade level and are rarely preserves beyond a 12 month period. Infantry units are, however, requires to take part in the "Tickle Competition" for which results are maintained by the Army Rifle Association (ARA). This competition is based on APWT results on the SA 80 and the Light Support Weapon (LSW).

Results for the period 1989–92 are attached at Annex C. Those for Training Year 1992/93 have not yet been collated by the ARA and Headquarters Directorate of Infantry.

This data shows that Infantry shooting standards appear to remain at a constant level. The results in the LSW Match indicate that the standard in LSW shooting is below that of the SA 80.

Q3. The Committee would be assisted by copies of the Army Collective Training Strategy Paper and the Development Plan for major training areas.

A3. The Army Collective Training Strategy Paper is an internal working document, which is not our practice to release. However a paper is being prepared which summarises its broad provisions and conclusions.

The major development projects required on Army training areas and arranges to meet the future demands of both the Field Army and the Army Training Organisation in UK are still under consideration and no final decisions have been made.

Q4. It would be helpful to have details on purchases and disposals of training land over the past 10 years and notes on Holcombe Moor, the Cnewr Estate, the Coombe feature, Rowborough Down, additions at Nesscliff.

A4. Details of purchases and disposals of training land are only held centrally covering the last five years. Details for the past 10 years are attached.

*Not printed.

1. Holcombe Moor

Holcombe Moor lies approximately 14 miles to the North West of Manchester. Additional land was purchased from Lord Clitheroe (Clitheroe Land) and Dunham builder (Simon's Sundial) to extend Dry Training Capabilities.

(a) Clitheroe Land

371 hectares of moorland was purchased from Lord Clitheroe when a two year "Option to Purchase" expired in December 1989.

A Planning Appeal by Public Inquiry to introduce Military Training took place at the commencement of the two year option period, but fundings were not made known until after the December 1989 purchase date.

The original purchase made to provide additional facilities for the increase number of Service personnel that would be based in the North West; many of them as a result of a planned increase in the strength of the Territorial Army. Since then, there have been dramatic changes in the disposition and deployment of military units. We looked carefully at whether Holcombe Moor would be suitable for the Army's training requirements as they are now foreseen and concluded that for a number of reasons the additional Clitheroe land would not be suitable; we therefore withdrew from any further effort to secure rights to train over it. A key concern was that even had we persisted with the Inquiry into our use of the land the training value of it would almost certainly have been diminished by constraints on the type of activity that would have been permitted. In August 1992 the decision was made to dispose of the land.

Negotiations are proceeding to sell this land to the National Trust, and hopefully these will be positively concluded within the next few weeks.

During the Public Inquiry a statement was made that 11 hectares of the Clitheroe Land near the Peel Monument would possibly be made available to the Local Authority as a public amenity for those visiting the monument. However, Bury Council would rather see the whole going to National Trust in the hope that in this way their use of the monument land could be gained at no cost.

(b) Simon's Sundial

Approximately four hectares of land with derelict cottage purchased partly by Private Treaty, and partly by negotiation including an "Option to Purchase" which expired in April 1989.

Although this land is not used for training, its proximity to the range firing point means that it forms an effective buffer zone which is essential for public safety and which also helps reduce the noise nuisance resulting from the use of pyrotechnics and blanks during dry training. In addition the Army see the area as a buffer against possible commercial pressures and to separate the new Range Area from nearby residences. The final decision concerning the future of this land has yet to be taken.

2. Cnewr Estate

Since 1976 the Estate has been used for adventurous military training on an *ad hoc* basis by permission of the owners and without payment. Similar use is made of much other land in the National Park including that owned by the National Park Authority. Such military use is not incompatible with farming or public access and indeed there are two permissive public paths across the Cnewr Estate.

Concern about military use of the Estate was raised after the owners decided not to conclude an open access agreement which they had been negotiating with the National Park. MOD did not influence this decision. At the same time the owners of the Cnewr Estate made approaches to MOD to see if the ongoing military use could be put on a more formal basis with possibly some payment. One meeting took place to explore the possibilities but no decisions were reached and no financial offer made. No significant increase in the type or amount of military use has been proposed. In view of the MOD Declaration of Commitment to the National Parks, any negotiations must involve involve the National Park in order to ensure compatibility of objectives. The National Park Authority have been asked to take part in negotiations.

The current position is that military use of the Cnewr Estate continues as before, on an *ad hoc* basis, and MOD awaits the commencement of three-way negotiations (with the owners and the National Park Authority) to explore the possibility of a more formal agreement with the Estate.

3. The Coombe Feature—Salisbury Plain Training Area

The Coombe Feature is an area of some 1,110 acres (450 hectares) comprising two farms. It projected into the training area and prevented the full utilisation of the eastern area of the Plain for training as can be seen from the attached map at Annex D*. The detrimental effect was recognised in the Report of the Defence Lands Committee 1971–73 (the Nugent Report) where a recommendation was made that this land should be acquired by the Department if it became available on the open market.

Until the late 1980s the two owners refused to consider a sale to MOD. Because of the importance of the Feature it was decided that the Defence Land Agent (DLA) should try to negotiate an acceptable price. It is the

*Not printed.

Department's policy to avoid using compulsory powers and to seek to acquire by agreement. In this case it was, exceptionally, agreed to offer to purchase on the same basis as compulsory purchase. This meant that the owners would receive the open market value for the land plus compensation for farm loss/disturbance, injurious affection and fees, etc. Agreement with the owner was subsequently negotiated and supported by the District Valuer. Approval was conditional on the Department disposing of a broadly equivalent acreage of training land as soon as it could. Three areas of land have been identified; two freehold areas, Oakhanger Farm, Bordon (431 acres) and Woolfords Farm, Hankley Common (83 acres), and an area of 820 acres at Roborough Down, Dartmoor held on licence. The freehold land is in the process of disposal and the Roborough Down land will be relinquished when the existing agreement terminates in September 1994. In order to obtain full benefit from the Coombe Feature acquisition agreement also was reached with two tenant farmers to convert 305 acres (123 hectares) from full agricultural tenancy to licensed land. The package will enable more effective use of the training areas to be made disproportionate to the size of the area acquired. The overall cost of the package was £4 million.

4. ROBOROUGH DOWN

This training area, amounting some 820 acres, is situated at the Southern end of Roborough Down on either side of the A386. MOD has had a licence for training over Roborough Down since 1946, although training was probably carried out over the same area during the Second World War. The current six year licence expires in September 1994. Little, if any, training is now carried out on the site pending expiry of the licence.

5. ADDITIONS AT NESSCLIFF TRAINING AREA—NEAR SHREWSBURY

Nesscliff Training Area is a District Facility extending to 688 hectares comprising two major blocks of land, the southern area fronting onto the River Severn. The area is used for Dry Training purposes extensively throughout the year, supported by Hutted Camp (circa 1940) which is centrally located providing accommodation for 410 Officers, 55 Senior NCOs and 499 Other Ranks.

The only live firing which occurs is on the Southern Training Area where a Grenade Range Facility has been constructed. Within the Northern Training Area a FIBUA has been created based around the original farmstead known as Acksea Farm. The majority of the Training Area is let for concurrent agricultural purposes and in the Financial Year 92/93 produced an income of £65K. Integrated with the agricultural use and to improve the Tactical Training Value a programme of aforestation continues, with mixed conifers/hardwoods, now covering an area of 65 hectares.

In the mid 1980s it was decided that the Army should seek to acquire land adjacent to Nesscliff on an ''opportunity'' basis when it became available and at the commencement of the Acquisition Programme Nesscliff extended to 520 hectares. Clearly the Acquisition Policy at Nesscliff has been extremely successful and has considerably enhanced the tactical capabilities for use by the Infantry in development terms and by ongoing enhancement provided a variety of Training situations for visiting Units. The acquisition have also increased accessibility to the River Severn for watermanship and other water based training.

In all 170 hectares have been acquired at a total cost of £659,000.

Individual acquisitions comprised:

(a) The Warner Land

This land immediately adjoined Nesscliff Training Camp and purchase gave direct access from the Camp into the Training Area.

This land is also within the central core between the two blocks of Training Area and the long term aim is to acquire the intervening land holdings.

(b) The Price Land

This land adjoined the Southwest corner of the Training Area, has river frontage, and together with the two further areas of land acquired from Mr Jones and the Myerscough Trust in 1989 formed a very useful enlargement to the Southern Training Area.

(c) The Bradford Land

This land together with a farmstead and woodland adjoined the Training Area in the north where it has been extremely narrow and restrictive. The established woodland was also attractive being immediately suitable for Training purposes.

(d) The Jones and Myerscough Trust Land

This adjoins the Price land affording a further useful extension of the Training Area with river frontage.

(e) The Pugh Land

This adjoined the Bradford land and purchase enabled the woodland block to become surrounded by MOD freehold ownership.

(f) The Caviapen Land

This land was adjacent to the Northern Training Area. The acquisition again added width to improve mobility within the area.

Three copies of the public access guides are attached for the Committee's use.*

Q5. It would also be helpful to have copies of the public access guides to the Otterburn Training Area and the Coquet Valley.

A5. Copies of each of the public access guides to the Otterburn Training Area and The Coquet Valley are attached.*

ANNEX A   **IGDT Command and Staff Structure**

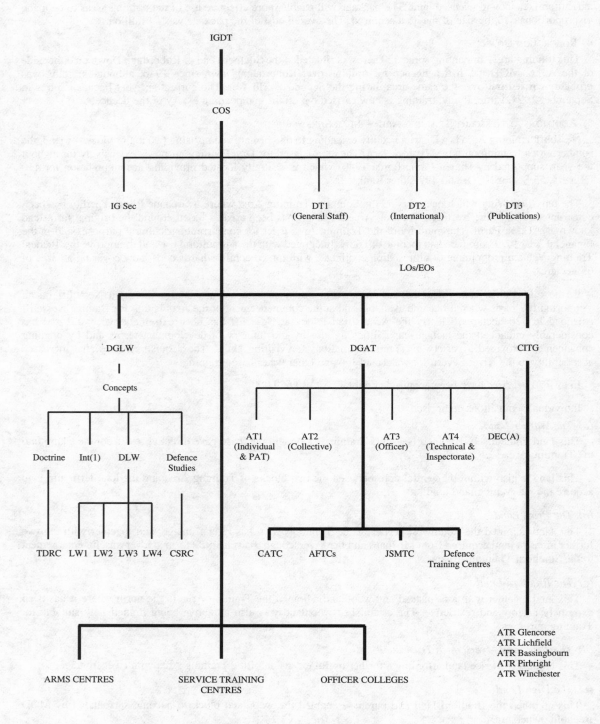

(1) This branch is headed by the Director of Intelligence for the formulation of intelligence doctrine.

ANNEX B**

ANNEX C

Tickle Statistics

Year/statistic	89/90	90/91	91/92
Total Inf Bns in orbat	55	55	55
Total Inf Bns participating	33	27	21
% participating	60	49	38
SA80 participants	4,079	3,080	2,640
Failures	614	549	329
% failures	15	18	13
LSW participants	1,055	612	603
Failures	546	272	300
% failures	49	45	50

ANNEX D Not Printed.

ANNEX E

The Army's Collective Training Strategy: A Summary

1. The Army Training Organisation provides new recruits to the Army with the skills required to take their place in the Field Army. First, in the initial training group, recruits are taught a common military syllabus after which they pass to their respective Arm or Service centre for Phase 2 training which fits them to take their place in their first unit. Subsequently all members of the Army will return to the training organisation for Phase 3, or career, training designed to fit them for promotion or to pass on new skills.

2. However, the Army is more than the sum of well trained individuals. To be effective individuals must join together for collective training. Collective training works at several levels. It involves the training of crews and detachments, sub-units and units and lastly formations in the conduct of tactical operations.

3. Some units such as those deploying to Northern Ireland on operational tours or others with a short readiness time need to be training so that they are immediately capable of undertaking certain military tasks. However, with an increased warning time overall there is no requirement to maintain all units at such a level. We have therefore considered what collective training standards must be set and what training activity needs to be undertaken to provide a general level of capability across the Army.

4. At the highest level SACEUR has already indicated the framework for exercises at formation level and further, more detailed work is being carried out on the specific requirements for formations in the ARRC.

5. Alongside the need to train in the NATO context the Army must also be able to take part in Joint Service ("Purple") exercises, to test and assess the ability to project and sustain forces overseas in support of national interests. The requirements for the Army to maintain a strategic reserve capability to undertake a range of operations beyond the NATO area was endorsed by "Options for Change". Purple exercises envisage a field training exercise every four years and a command post exercise in each of the other three. Formations and units earmarked for this role should aim to exercise at this frequency and effects will be made to ensure that there is no conflict between NATO and Purple commitments.

6. Units should aim to train in the special to arm skills required for their primary role every year. The Chain of Command will need to direct such training towards specific collective training objectives, concentrating on the unit's primary role. In time, the Combined Arms Tactical Trainer planned to enter service in 1998 will, by practising procedures, tactics and drills prepare units in a simulated environment to obtain the maximum benefits of deployment to field training. Tactical Engagement Simulation employing direct and, later, area effects simulators to be introduced in early 1994 will in turn create greater tactical realism and awareness during training.

7. Battle groups and battalion groups are the basic building blocks of combined arms operations. The value of such groups will only be realised by training. The Chain of Command will lay down a cycle of collective training objectives. Training will be undertaken to ensure that units are sufficiently prepared to allow their deployment at the beginning of any warning period. In the event of an unforeseen operational task arising at shorter notice than anticipated the unit best able to meet the commitment will be readily known to the Chain of Command. It will also allow training not recently practised to be known. As a result training during the warning period can be directed more accurately and more effectively.

8. Commanders and their staffs will also need to train. The Higher Formation Trainer will enter service in 1994 and will meet ARRC computer assisted exercise requirements. This will provide formation headquarters with a tool to rehearse manoeuvre warfare in an airland environment. The Brigade and Battle Group Trainer, already in

service will train brigade commanders and their staff in the conduct of the manoeuvre battle at brigade level and below.

9. Formation Commanders will be responsible for deciding the operations and phases of war upon which they wish their subordinate formations to concentrate in the coming year. The Chain of Command will then set collective training objectives. At the start of the training year a commander will choose those training tasks upon which he wishes his units to concentrate and they will then become the unit's objectives for the year. This will be determined by the unit's role, state of training and commitments. The Commander will then assess the unit's performance during the training year.

ANNEX F

Army Training Land Acquisitions 1982/83 to 1991/92 (over 20 hectares in area)

Financial Year	Number of Acquisitions	Area (hectares)
1982–83	3	120
1983–84	3	247
1984–85	3	374
1985–86	13	799
1986–87	19	2,134
1987–88	16	2,360
1988–89	7	282
1989–90	12	941
1990–91	0	0
1991–92	4	834
Total	80	8,091

Army Training Land Disposals 1982/83 to 1991/92 (over 20 hectares in area)

Financial Year	Number of Acquisitions	Total Area (hectares)
1982–83	1	85
1983–84	2	69
1984–85	Nil	Nil
1985–86	Nil	Nil
1986–87	2	210
1987–88	1	104
1988–89	2	241
1989–90	1	63
1990–91	1	39
1991–92	1	43
Total	1	854

2. Memorandum submitted by the Ministry of Defence answering the Committee's Questions on Army Training following the Oral Evidence taken on 7 July 1993 (28 October 1993)

Q1. It would be helpful to have as detailed a breakdown as is available of the IGDT HLB, showing also identifiable training expediture borne on other budgets; and the extent of IGDT's responsibilities for Forces outside the UK.

A1. IGDT is a Higher Level Budget holder in the C in C UKLF Top Level Budget, with a FY 93/94 allocation of £526 million. There are 11 Intermediate Higher Level Budgets (IHLBs), which each have a number of subordinate basic level budgets, and 6 Stand Alone Basic Level Budgets (BLBs). This breakdown is shown below, with the number of BLBs within each IHLB shown in brackets.

Intermediate Higher Level Budgets
Director of Infantry (5)
Director Royal Armoured Corps (5)
Director Royal Artillery (6)
Engineer in Chief (Army) (5)
Signal Officer in Chief (Army) (3)
Director Army Air Corps (2)
Director General Logistic Support (Army) (7)
Director General Engineering Support (Army) (6)
Director General Adjutant General's Corps (3)
Director General Army Medical Services (2)
Commander Initial Training Group (5)
Chief of Staff HQDT (2)

Stand Alone Basic Level Budgets
Royal Military Academy, Sandhurst
Royal Military College of Science
Staff College
Defence Animal Centre
Army Field Training Centres
Combined Arms Training Centre

Funding is allocated in three broad areas, Pay (£319 million), Movements (£6 million) and Administration Costs (£201 million).

Training expenditure is borne on a number of other budgets. For example the UKLF School of Adventurous Training, in Ripon, forms part of the Eastern District HLB within CinC UKLF's TLB. The British Army Training Unit Suffield (BATUS) in Canada is currently funded from CinC BAOR's budget. The costs of jungle training in Belize are not currently separable from the overall costs of the Garrison which is funded from the VCDS budget. The cost of jungle training in Brunei are met from the HQ British Forces Hong Kong budget. Much Field Army activity—both in UKLF and BAOR—could be also be described as training.

IGDT's responsibility for Forces outside UK is largely limited to that of sponsor and policy maker. For example, the Training Team Brunei provides a focus for jungle training within the Army, and develops jungle warfare doctrine with HQ British Forces Belize and our allies. This unit is sponsored by the Combined Arms Training Centre, a part of the IGDT's area, but is administered and funded by HQBF Hong Kong. IGDT is also the sponsor of a number of British Liaison Officers overseas.

Q2. The Committee has asked for elucidation of the reference to Crickhowell in para 716 of SDE 93.

A2. The original proposals for interim infantry training, pending location to a single site were announced on 10 March 1992 and envisaged the use of Crickhowell as one of the interim training locations. Subsequent work identified Catterick as the preferred single long term location for Infantry training. The available capacity at Catterick meant that it would no longer be necessary to make use of Crickhowell in the interim for Infantry training. This was announced on 16 December 1992.

Q3. Further to Qq2160ff, it would be helpful to have an elucidation of the figure of 15,700 referred to, including the extent to which officer numbers are included, and an example of the possible additional accommodation requirement referred to at Q2160.

A3. The figure of 15,700 represents the Director of Army Recruiting's estimate of the number of soldiers the Army might be able to recruit in the year 95/96. Forecast recruiting figures are reviewed twice each year by the Standing Committee on Army Manpower Forecast (SCAMF). The figure of 15,700 does not include officers and this number could be accommodated in existing accommodation. In the event that this did not prove to be the case alternative accommodation would need to be found.

Q4. Details of the graduate/non-graduate breakdown of the first Common Commissioning Courses at Sandhurst were sought (Q2170–1). It would also be helpful to have a note on any proposals for changes at RMCS Shrivenham, in the light of the information on the CST review provided on 8 July.

A4. The breakdown of graduates and non-graduates on the first Commissioning Course run at RMAS (from Sep 92–Aug 93) is as follows:

(1) Graduates – 210.
(2) Non-Graduates – 48.

These are no proposals for changes at RMCS in the light of the CST review.

Q5. A note on recent figures for the adventurous training budget would be helpful, and on proposals for Kiel.

A5. The majority of adventurous training is conducted at unit level using vehicles, rations and fuel from the unit. The cost of this is contained within the unit's budget and is not separately identifiable.

Additional funding to provide clothing, textiles, equipment and technical training in support of adventurous training, amounted, in FY 92/93, to £2.2 million.

The total cost of maintaining the Joint Service Mountain Training Centres in FY 92/93 was £2.2 million.

HQ BAOR have now completed a study into the Kiel Training centre. The centre is to be restructured and will become, by April 1994, the Adventurous Sail Training Centre, Kiel. Under this restructuring, and in line with the drawdown in BAOR, some 5 military and 11.5 civilian posts will no longer be required.

Q6. 1993–94 figures for the Tickle Test would be helpful: and available figures on relative personal weapons proficiency results as between different arms and Corps (Qq2199–2201).

A6. The figures for the 1993–94 Tickle Test have not yet been collated, (and will be forwarded separately when completed). The results of the 1992/93 Test were published by the Army Rifle Association in June 1993. A copy of this document is attached.*

The average pass rate achieved by each Arm and Service in the Annual Personal Weapons Test for the training period 92–93 is shown, by percentage, in the table below:

Arms/Service	Pass Rate
Royal Armoured Corps	85.75%
Royal Artillery	78%
Royal Engineers	77.4%
Royal Signals	88.23%
Infantry	98%
Army Air Corps	91%
Royal Logistic Corps	89.25%
Royal Electrical & Mechanical Engineers	86.5%
Adjutant Generals' Corps	79.2%
Intelligence Corps	86%
Army Medical Services	81.8%
Army Average Pass Rate	85.86%

Q7. Further to Qq2179 and 2194ff and para 754 of SDE 93, the Committee would be assisted by details of the current differences in required standards of physical fitness and strength as between men and women.

A7. The physical requirements for each of the military employment groups are currently under study. The current basic fitness test for Women is also being re-examined. Currently there are two areas where differing standards of fitness are applied:

(a) *Recruit Training*—during recruit training trainees are assessed for physical development progress. The physiological gender differences are reflected in the standards required which are shown in the table below:

Male

Test	Introduction	Interim	Final
Heaves	2	4	6
Sit up Test	1 Min (20 Reps)	2 Mins (42 Reps)	3 Mins (65 Reps)
1.5 Mile Run	11 Mins 30 Secs	11 Minutes	10 Mins 30 Secs

Female

Test	Introduction	Interim	Final
Heaves	4	8	12
Sit up Test	1 Min (20 Reps)	2 Mins 50 Secs (38 Reps)	2 Mins 40 Secs (58 Reps)
1.5 Mile Run	14 Mins 15 Secs	13 Mins 30 Secs	12 Mins 50 Secs

*Not printed.

(b) *Basic Fitness Test (BFT)*—The different standards set for males and females are shown below.

Basic Fitness Test for Men

Ser	Test	Conditions	Standards
1	Part 1 Run and Walk 1.5 miles squadded.	1. On level group—good running surface. 2. Dress PT kit + pullover or similar garment in cold weather and training shoes. 3. Part 1 Squads to be controlled running and walking to arrive at 1.5 mile mark in 15 minutes exactly.	1. Both parts of test must be completed within the time limit shown below: Part 2 — Within 29 or under — 10 Mins 30–34 yrs — 11 Mins 35–39 yrs — 12 Mins 40–44 yrs — 13 Mins 45–49 yrs — 14 Mins
	Part 2 Run 1.5 miles as an individual (best effort).	4. Part 2 To follow Part 1 without a break.	
2	Alternative Test for Men Over 40. Run and Walk 3 miles as an individual.	1. Dress: As above.	Within Time Limits 40–44 yrs — 28 Mins 45–49 yrs — 29 Mins

Basic Fitness Test for Women

Ser	Test	Conditions	Standards
1	Women under 40. Part 1 March/Jog 0.5 mile squadded.	1. On level group—good running surface. 2. Dress PT kit or tracksuit and training shoes. 3. Part 1 Squads to be controlled to complete the 0.5 mile in 16 minutes exactly.	1. Both parts of test must be completed within the time limit shown below: Part 2 — Within 29 or under — 13 Mins 45 Secs 30–34 yrs — 14 Mins 30 Secs 35–39 yrs — 15 Mins 15 Secs
	Part 2 Run 1.5 miles as an individual (best effort).	4. Part 2 To follow Part 1 without a break.	
2	Women Over 40. Walk 2 miles	1. Dress: As above.	Within 28 Minutes.

Q8. Pursuant to Qq2216, details of Training Ammunition level would be helpful, together with other equivalent objective measurements of training inputs or outputs.

A8. The Training Ammunition Level is determined from the following components:—

(a) *Individual*—Every soldier is required to maintain a basic standard of personal weapon training. The individual training requirement is calculated on the manpower strength and weapon holdings of each unit. Differentials are made where necessary—for instance a sniper will require more training ammunition than a driver. Training output in terms of weapon handling proficiency is measured in the annual Personal Weapons Test (APWT).

(b) *Unit*—The Compendium of Unit Collective Training Tasks details the levels of training which units are expected to achieve in terms and content. The unit training ammunition requirement is therefore a calculation of what is physically required to meet these targets taking into account the operational readiness of each unit and its role in the orbat. As the use of infantry and common user ammunition for low-level training is difficult to predict accurately, pools of training ammunition are provided in each command to enable resources to be used more efficiently. Training output is reported on annually in the unit Operational Evaluation (OPEVAL).

(c) *Course*—Courses held in recognised training establishments are based on specified training objectives where performance is measured on how well the objectives are met. The courses of all the major establishments are subject to constant scrutiny by Training Development Teams who monitor output and recommend changes where necessary. The course ammunition requirement is calculated according to the number and type of courses authorised by Arms Directorates.

The measurement of training outputs is being considered with the Defence Operational Analysis Centre.

Q9. The Committee has asked for a breakdown of the principal costs of overseas exercises, showing separately countries imposing per capita charges, and including a breakdown of the estimated £2.5 million cost of Belize training. It would also be helpful to have details of funding arrangements for Red Stripe (Q2237) including an explanation of the rationale for FCO funding, and the basis (additional or full) on which charge are made.

A9. The principal costs of overseas exercises, which vary from country to country area comprise:

    (i) Movement costs—to and from host country and internally.
   (ii) Fuel—liquid and solid.
  (iii) Accommodation.
  (iv) Laundry.
   (v) Telephone.
  (vi) Local purchases.
 (vii) Conservancy—for example disposal of rubbish and swill.
(viii) Payment of locally employed civilians.
  (ix) Open vote for rations, medical and dental charges—paid for only in emergencies.
   (x) Infrastructure costs—where applicable for property and maintenance.

The estimated costs (£ million) of training in Belize in 1995–96 (the first full year with a full training presence) are as follows:

Pay	1.964
Movement costs	0.076
Administration	1.198
Total	3.238
less receipts (eg recovery of electricity charges)	0.064
	3.174

Exercise Red Stripe/Calypso Hop is an annual 4 week minor unit exercise between sub-units from the United Kingdom and the Jamaica Defence Force (JDF). Each exercise also involves the exchange of up to 20 tri-service personnel. The FCO part-fund the exercise as a means of providing support to the development of the JDF. The exercise is funded on an extra cost basis with no capitation charges raised. These are borne by UKLF.

Q10. It would be helpful to have details (including costs and timescales), as briefed to the Committee earlier this year at Warminster, of the planned SPTA, Otterburn and Catterick upgrades; and the reason for the exclusion of the proposed improvements from the transitional works programme.

A10. The costs of improvements to Salisbury Plain Training Area (SPTA), Otterburn Training Area (OTA) and Catterick Training Area (CTA) are still being assessed.

It was decided within the Department that the development of Army Training Land could not be funded by Transitional Works Funds which are time limited.

Q11. Further to Qq2266–7, it would be helpful to have a paper on individual and unit training in the TA at all phases, in comparison with that for the Regular Army, and including information on TA exercises in the UK and abroad.

A11. A paper is attached (Annex A).

ANNEX A

A comparison between Territorial and Regular Army Training
(A paper by Director General Army Training)

BACKGROUND

1. The House of Commons Defence Committee has requested a comparison of Regular and Territorial Army (TA) training. HQDT has been closely involved with Directorate of Reserve Forces and Cadets (DRFC) and HQ UKLF in determining the optimum way ahead for TA training. As a result of the TA restructuring, ECAB directed that the training of officers should remain unchanged, but consideration should be given to restructuring the training of TA soldiers. A Training Efficiency Study was carried out in 1991 and a number of recommendations were made and improvements introduced. The key changes included the introduction of TA Brigade Concentrations which has been a great success and the TA Training Instruction is presently being rewritten to put in place other improvements.****

AIM

2. The aim of this paper is to provide a comparison between TA and Regular Army Training.

CONSTRAINTS ON TA TRAINING

3. When comparing TA with regular Army Training there are a number of important constraints which must be taken into account. They are:

(a) Time available for training currently averages out at 36 training days per man per year. The target is for an average of 40 days a year.

(b) ****

(c) ****

PHASES OF TRAINING

4. Army training is divided into three phases. The requirements for each Phase are tabulated below:

Phase	Regular Army	TA
(a)	(b)	(c)
1	The basic 10 week common military syllabus for recruits irrespective of capbadge and including females. Conducted at the Army Training Regiments.	The common military Syllabus (TA) (currently in two phases) is conducted as follows: (a) Part 1—by TA units of the Field Army. (b) Part 2—by the ATO (15 Days).
2	The employment or Special to Arm training designed to take his/her place in their first field unit.	Special to Arm Training aimed at making the TA recruit "Fit for Role".
3	The progressive career training that is given to a soldier throughout his career.	As for Regular Army.

****

INDIVIDUAL SOLDIER TRAINING

5. *Aim.* The aim of individual training in the TA is to prepare all ranks for their mobilisation roles. Training objectives for the individual, irrespective of specialisation, reflect the fact that members of the TA are soldiers first and specialists second. Despite the current financial restrictions on Man Training Days (MTD) to an average of 36 days per year, basic individual skills and minor tactics are not neglected. This ensures that individuals have the chance to qualify for their training bounty at the earliest opportunity.

6. ****

7. ****

8. ****

9. *Staff Training.* A comparison of Command and Staff training is at Annex B.[1]

COLLECTIVE TRAINING

10. Collective training is related directly to the mobilisation role of the unit, in line with Regular Army training. Training can range from weekend exercises, use of specialist training facilities, ie Battlegroup Trainers to enable the Commander to train his HQ in drills, procedures and tactics, and major exercises in the UK and abroad. There are also plans to give the TA greater access to simulation training.

11. Currently TA Battalions conduct an annual Camp of 15 days as a unit, either on their own or as part of a concentration coordinated at Brigade level. In comparison the Regular Army exercise on average, commitments allowing, twice a year as a unit in a formation exercise or on overseas training. A comparison of the number of formation level exercises which had or will have TA participation is shown below:

Year	Regular	TA
93–94	16	11
94–95	16	8

[1] Not printed.

12. Additionally, the table below compares the Regular Army and TA participation in overseas exercises (not including AMF(L) and BAOR based exercises) between 1993 and 1995:

Year	Unit Level	Sub-unit level
93–94	Regular 9	Regular 18
	TA 1	TA 8
94–95	Regular 8	Regular 20
	TA 6	TA 8

13.   Other unit level exercises include regular AMF(L) exercises in Europe and TA annual camps in BAOR. Current participation is:

(a) *AMF(L).* On average there are 3 regular unit level exercises per year

(b) *TA Camps in BAOR.* Deployments to BAOR vary from year to year. In 93/94 there were none, however for 94–95 nine are currently programme to take place.

CONCLUSIONS

14. Constrained by time a TA soldier is expected to take his place in the ORBAT alongside his Regular counterpart having had up to 90 days post mobilisation training.

15. The ATO commitment to TA training is primarily to meet the requirements of the Common Military Syllabus TA (CMS TA, Part 2) and Phases 2 and 3 specialist training.

16. A Potential Officer in the TA Officer can reach the 2 week RMAS commissioning course via the Akehurst scheme, Ex FAST TRACK, or through the UOTC. Time constraints do not allow TA O/Cdts to receive as much personal and leadership skills as their Regular counterparts.

****

3. Extract from a memorandum submitted by the Ministry of Defence in response to the Committee's request for an update on Army Training (27 January 1994)

Q1.(i) Brigadier Mountford's study into the recruitment of young servicemen and women (Q2154).

A1.(i) The Mountford Study considered the effects of combining 16 year old recruits with more mature recruits in the same training system.

The Single Entry (SE) system was introduced on 1 September 1993, as indicated by the then Minister (AF) in the House on 16 December 1992 (cols WA 335–336). Implicit in the adoption of the SE was the termination of special arrangements for age groups formerly categorised as Junior Leader or Young Soldier: from the introduction of SE men and women aged 16 years and upwards were to be treated identically. From that date, all new soldier entrants to the Army, less apprentices, Royal Irish and Gurkhas, have carried out their initial training at their respective Army Training Regiments (ATR).

Recruits to be trained under the SE system are required to attend a Recruit Selection Centre (RSC), to ensure that those enlisted are sufficiently mature to undertake recruit training and are suitable for employment in their selected Arm or Service once they have attended Phase Two (Special to Arm) training. One RSC has already been established at Lichfield and the RSCs at Pirbright and Glencorse will have opened by the end of January 1994. All under 17 year olds applying to join will have undergone recruit selection and the proportion of 17 year olds and over who will have done so will increase as those accepted, but deferred prior to the introduction of the new system, are called forward for training.

Initially some 800 to 1,000 recruits under age 16 years and 9½ months will be accepted per year: around 300 will join RAC, RA, RE and Infantry; the balance will join the technical Corps. These numbers will be reviewed later as experience of SE is gained. To date some 260 16 year olds have been selected for recruit training. There is insufficient information available as yet to determine whether their failure rate is significantly different from that of their more adult counterparts. None has arrived in the Field Army yet.

As a result of the study all recruits will receive a brochure, from the Director Army Recruiting, with joining instructions describing and showing the major steps of Phase 1 training, and once the recruit has started Phase 1 training a contract letter will be sent to the next of kin.

As a general principle, but excepting very small units, Phase 1 recruits will be accommodated in "recruit areas", with trained soldiers in clearly separated accommodation. Recruits undergoing Phase 2 training will be accommodated in "recruit areas" within which:

 (i) Trained soldiers do not share rooms with the recruits.

(ii) NCOs are accommodated in separate rooms in sufficient numbers and in such a manner to ensure that recruits are properly supervised and have access to advice and guidance.

Phase 2 recruits are in a sub-unit clearly identified and properly organised for recruits undergoing training with a command structure with clear responsibilities for all non-instructional matters.

Soldiers under age 18 may not buy or consume alcohol: non alcoholic recreation facilities have been made available where practical, and wherever possible, recruits undergoing Phase 1 and Phase 2 training are to have the use of bars in Junior Ranks Clubs from which trained soldiers are excluded. (Although exceptions are granted to small units or large units with relatively few trained soldiers.)

Some additional PT instructors have been established at each ATR to allow for the introduction of simple streaming by age and physical ability during PT periods and to support remedial platoons. The establishment of these remedial platoons for recruits who have failed a stage of training or in the event of injury has been increased for the Single Entry.

The auxiliary welfare agencies in the Army Training Regiments have been enhanced and a clear welfare focus has been identified for Phase 2 recruits.

A review of the Single Entry is to be undertaken in February 1994.

Q1.(ii) The study into the future of RASAM (Q2182).

A1.(ii) This study is now complete and the conclusions were announced by means of a written Parliamentary answer on 18 January.

Q1.(iii) The study into the Army's future requirements for jungle training (Q2247).

A1.(iii) A study paper has been written and is currently being staffed within the department.

Q1.(iv) The report into the future requirements for training land (Q2261).

A1.(iv) Work has been put in train to define the training land required by the Army (the Total Training requirement) and to match this against the Army's holding of training land (Total Training Capacity). This study is being assisted by a civilian consultant whose task is to provide a computer software programme to match the Total Training Requirement (TTR) against the Total Training Capacity (TTC). The study is expected to be complete by Summer 1994, with the computer programme available for use in future years.

4. Letter to the Clerk of the Committee from the Private Secretary to the Secretary of State for Defence on the costs of Training in Belize (10 December 1993)

Thank you for your letter of 3 November in which the Committee asked for a breakdown of the costs for full-year Belize training.

The full costs of the resident support unit in Belize, once withdrawal has taken place, will be:

Pay	*£ million*
Service Pay	1.774
Locally Employed Civilians	0.190
Administration	
Stores	0.025
Clothing and Textiles	0.035
Fuel	0.187
General Admin	0.019
Communications	0.126
Local Purchase	0.011
Civilian Hospital Costs	0.170
Property Management	0.400
Local hirings/Contracts	0.225

The annual cost of units deploying to Belize for training will depend on a number of factors including numbers, frequency, and duration of deployments.

5. Parliamentary Question and Answer on competition shooting (18 January 1994)

Tuesday 18 January 1994

Sir James Spicer
To ask the Secretary of State for Defence, if he will make a statement on the Army's policy on competition shooting.

Mr Hanley: A major review of the Army's policy on training in shooting skills, including the role of the Regular Army Skill-at-Arms Meeting (the RASAM) has recently been completed. The RASAM, which involved eight shooting days, was highly manpower intensive. Against the background of the Army's very heavy commitments at a time of restructuring and reducing numbers, I have taken the view that RASAM should be replaced by a one-day event, to be known as the Regular Army Queen's Medal Competition. The new competition will continue to encourage excellence in Army shooting and meet the terms governing the award of The Queen's Medal. Competitors will be selected from Divisional and District meetings, to be held under new guidelines issued by the Inspector General, Doctrine and Training. These guidelines will be designed to ensure a high standard of marksmanship throughout each Army unit, and that resources are available to improve the less proficient as well as enhance the skills of those who are already excellent shots.

The Royal Navy, the Royal Marines and the Royal Air Force will continue to hold their own central Skill-at-Arms Meeting, overlapping with the new Army competition. This will be run by the Royal Air Force on behalf of the other Services. International competitors will be able to take part, as before, in the various Service and National Rifle Association competitions as well as in the International Match on the last day of the Meeting.

The Territorial Army Skill-at-Arms Meeting and the Combined Cadet Force (Schools) and the Inter-Service Cadet Rifle Meeting will take place as before.

6. Memorandum submitted by the Ministry of Defence answering the Committee's questions following the visit to Portsmouth (6 December 1993)

Q1. Following its visit to Portsmouth on 21 October 1993, the Committee has sought information on three matters:

(a) *The programme, including costs, for the delivery of a Type 23 simulator training module to HMS DRYAD, and the operational implications for T23 crews operating with the new Command System at sea without having the benefit of previous shore training.*

(b) *The lessons learned from the DRYAD wargame on which the Committee was briefed, in particular those relating to equipment availability.*

(c) *The programme for the repair of the former Z berth at Portsmouth harbour, currently suffering from decaying concrete, and the operational implications of its condition.*

COMBINED TACTICAL TRAINER 5

A1.(a)(i) The Type 23 simulator training module to which the Committee refers is the Combined Tactical Trainer Stage 5 (CTT5); it will become an integral part of the School of Maritime Operations (SMOPS) at HMS DRYAD.

(ii) The programme for the procurement and installation of CTT5 is complex and will be supported by a Training Needs Analysis (TNA) which is taking into account previous work on the derivation of the operational need for this installation. It is expected that the programme will be as follows:

Oct–Dec 1992	—	Intramural stages of TNA
Dec 93/Jan 94	—	Invitations to tender for final stage of TNA
Jan 94	—	Place contract for final stage of TNA
Jun 94	—	TNA completed
Jun–Dec 94	—	Assess TNA and Project Definition proposals
Feb 95	—	Endorse Staff Requirement for Project Definition
Mar 95	—	Place contracts for Project Definition
Dec 95	—	Project Definition completed
Mar 96	—	Complete assessment of Project Definition
Jul 96	—	Re-endorse Staff Requirement for Development and Production
Sep 96	—	Place contract for Development and Production
Sep 98	—	In-Service Date.

(iii) The cost of CTT5 is estimated at some **** (at 1994 prices and inclusive of VAT). The bulk of expenditure is likely to fall within the Financial Years ****.

(iv) Since the Committee took evidence on the Command System itself, we have improved the situation in the Types 23. ****. To enable vessels to reach their full operation capability without recourse to frequent live exercises using other units—and to avoid the disruptive effects of almost continuous on-the-job training caused by trickle drafting—the crews will need the CTT5 training facility.

(v) The current arrangements are therefore transitional, but it is important to bear in mind that proficiency in the Type 23 is developed through a continuum of training processes undertaken as individuals advance, and it is relevant here that:

(a) a computer-based introductory skill trainer for operators of the Type 23 Command System will enter service in 1995; and

(b) a Type 23 Command System Skill Trainer (CSST) is being procured: its first phase will be ready for training in 1995 and a second phase 1997.

Although, in the early days, the ships will have a heavier than intended "on-the-job" (OJT) training load, and this may impact on overall operational effectiveness, sensible planning and management of OJT will enable units to establish and maintain a satisfactory level of operational capability.

PURPLE WARGAME

A1.(b) The Committee was briefed about the Purple Wargame to be played on 27–28 October at the Maritime Tactical School at HMS DRYAD. Collection of the detailed lessons learned is not expected to be completed before mid-December, but the initial indications are that the game was very profitable.

Z BERTH, NORTH CORNER JETTY

A1.(c)(i) The Z Berth referred to by the Committee is understood to be the North Corner Jetty. During the past five years, its usage as a Z Berth for nuclear-powered vessels has been confined to visiting US and French vessels; it has, however, been used by conventional RN vessels on a regular basis in its non-Z berth configuration. A recent survey of the structure of the jetty has confirmed the process of decay and the Portsmouth Navel Base authorities have ruled that it should no longer be used for any categories of berthing. The condition of the jetty has no operational implications for the Royal Navy in relation to Z berthing requirements, but its removal from use complicates the organisational arrangements for berthing within the Base and will pose some difficulties in the longer term.

Alternative Z berths are available at the Base's Middle Slip Jetty, 'C' Lock and No 3 Buoy. Foreign vessels may, however, be required to give more notice of visits, although short-notice demands for UK berths could be met at Devonport.

(ii) As regards repairs to the Jetty, the aim is that project work should begin in the coming financial year.

7. Memorandum submitted by the Ministry of Defence answering the Committee's questions on RN training following the oral evidence taken on 8 December 1993 (7 March 1994)

Q1. Further to Qq283–5, figures showing the extent of the recent problem of finding training berths for ratings would be helpful.

A1. The numbers of Royal Navy ratings awaiting their first sea draft after training at HMS RALEIGH and other training establishments varies according to their Branch. Figures for mid-January 1994 are as shown below:

(a) *Operations Branch.* 47 ratings. Average waiting time 3–4 months.

(b) *Marine Engineering Branch.* None.

(c) *Weapons Engineering Branch.* 15 WE Mechanics; this figures was due to fall to zero by end-January 1994. 99 WE Artificers; average wait 12 months.

(d) *Supply Branch.* None. It should, however, be noted that Supply Branch ratings tend to be drafted to one shore job of about 24 months before they go to their first ship.

(e) *Fleet Air Arm.* 238 AE Mechanics. This figure will fall to zero over the next 9 months as redundancies take effect.

(f) *Submarine Service.* 11 Artificers (ME and WE). Average wait 4–6 months.

2. With the exception of Air Engineering and Weapons Engineering personnel, the numbers of ratings awaiting First Sea Draft are unusually low because of recent recruiting cutbacks. The high number of AE Mechanics is caused by high recruitment in 1992 to meet the then expected requirements of the Merlin helicopter programme and a restructuring of the Air Engineering Branch. This requirement has since been reduced. The number of WE artificers reflects the fact that the recruiting level was high before the advent of "Options for Change" and, as a result, after 4 years' training, there is now a bulge of young artificers awaiting their first ship. This bulge will remain for at least the next 12 months as the training system continues to produce artificers as fast as they can be drafted to sea.

3. The following table shows the average waiting times before going to sea for various categories of new-entry rating for the calendar year 1993:

Category and Branch	Average number of weeks before First Sea Draft
Ops Branch	
AB(S)	8
AB(MW)	4
AB(M)	29
AB(EW)	14
AB(R)	8
WE Branch	
WEM(O)	29
WEM(R)	26
ME Branch	
MEM(M)	5
MEM(L)	11
Fleet Air Arm	
AEM	37
AEM(M)	46
AEM(L)	30
AEM(R)	26

Q2. It would be helpful to have statistical or analytical evidence on the value placed on staff college attendance as a precursor to higher command in the RN, if available in comparison with the other Services. (Qq296–9).

A2.(i) The aim of the RN Staff Course is to train Naval officers for service in the MOD, on Flag (Headquarters) Staffs and in command.

(ii) The selection of naval officers for staff training is made annually by the Directors of Naval Officer Appointments from among those senior Lieutenants and junior Lieutenant Commanders who are showing potential for higher rank. They are guided by recommendations made in annual Confidential Reports, including the specific recommendations for staff training made in those reports and, in the case of those who attend the Initial Staff Course, by recommendations made thereafter.

(iii) The following table indicates the number of naval officers, predominantly from the General List, in the rank of Lieutenant Commander, Commander and Captain, who have received staff training:

	Total general list	Initial Staff Course	%	RN Staff Course	%	Other[1] Staff Colleges	e+g as a proportion of b %
a	b	c	d	e	f	g	h
Captain	283	70	25	112	40	11	44
Commander	917	260	28	310	34	36	38
LT CDR	1,618	589	36	204[2]	13	20	14
Total	2,818	919	33	626	22	67	24

(iv) The ideal position for the Royal Navy would be to have every officer staff trained. This has been reinforced by the Officers' Study Group which has said that the aim is for all career officers to attend the Initial Staff Course and for all officers with the potential for promotion to Commander to attend the RN Staff Course or equivalent (blue pages vii and viii and white pages 11, 23 and 32 in the synopsis behind Enclosure 13a)[3]. Sea and other operational commitments, however, have hitherto denied some such officers that opportunity.

(v) The Army and the Royal Air Force value staff training very highly indeed and currently achieve percentage attendance levels broadly similar to those of the Royal Navy.

Q3. Further to Q306, the Committee has asked how Upper Yardmen selected by the Admiralty Interview Board for a BEng course at Southampton will achieve that qualification if their qualifications are judged insufficient by the University.

[1] Staff Colleges: RAF, Army, Joint Services, Foreign, Overseas Single Service, US Armed Forces, Australian Joint Services.
[2] Includes estimated 60 officers from last 2 RNSC courses, which have not been recorded on Management Information Systems to date.
[3] Not printed.

A3. School-leavers and Upper Yardmen (UY) will compete for places on the Engineering Sponsorship Scheme (ESS) on merit, as assessed by their AIB scores, having first achieved comparable academic results, either at A level or BTEC. As the RN expected to attract many school-leavers to this scheme, and many UY already achieve sufficiently high academic results, we currently see no need to provide assistance to those who do not meet the necessary academic standards. Thus, it is not the RN's intention to provide any additional academic training for ratings in the Engineering Branch who fail to achieve the level of BTEC passes necessary to meet the criteria for the Scheme.

Q4. It would be helpful to have an indication of the options under consideration for nuclear engineering training (Qq339–341).

A4.(i) The options for the possible location of the RN's nuclear engineering training facilities (the Department of Nuclear Science and Technology [DNST] and "JASON"—the Navy's low power nuclear reactor, both currently accommodated at Greenwich) considered in the Department's initial studies are as follows:

(a)   The Status Quo—DNST and JASON remain at RNC Greenwich.

(b)   The Status Quo, but dispose of JASON, hiring alternative reactor training facilities, either in the university or in the commercial sectors.

(c)   Relocate DNST to HMS SULTAN, Gosport, without JASON, hiring alternative reactor training facilities, either in the university or in the commercial sectors.

(d)   Relocate DNST and JASON to HMS SULTAN.

(e)   Relocate DNST to RMCS Shrivenham, Wiltshire, without JASON, hiring alternative reactor training facilities, either in the university or in the commercial sectors.

(f)   Relocate DNST and JASON to RMCS Shrivenham.

(g)   Relocate DNST to Manadon, Plymouth, without JASON, hiring alternative reactor training facilities.

(h)   Relocate DNST and JASON to Manadon.

(ii) As Mr Colvin pointed out during the HCDC Hearing on 8 December, it had been planned to relocate DNST and JASON to Manadon by April 1993. The recent decision concerning the transfer of first degree Engineer Officer education to Southampton University now means, however, that the site may be closed if alternative uses for it prove not to be cost-effective.

Q6. The Committee seeks details of past obligatory fitness testing, the standards then applied, the reasons for its termination, and the nature of the current voluntary scheme. (Qq350ff).

A6.(i) The merits of introducing compulsory Physical Fitness Tests (PFTs) have been considered twice, in 1976 and in 1993. On each occasion, it was decided that there was no clear operational requirement for a compulsory PFT; there was also a reluctance to increase the administrative burden on ships and the pressure on already stretched personnel.

(ii) In 1976, voluntary testing was introduced. It included the Harvard Step Test as a screening mechanism for individuals wishing to participate in the main PFT—a 1.5 mile timed run (details of the tests are set out at Annex A). The initiative failed largely because some Commanding Officers interpreted the guidance to mean that the tests were compulsory while others did not. Moreover, the Harvard Step Test was rarely used for its intended purpose and in some cases over-zealous management introduced an element of competition into the PFTs. Two men died during such fitness training, although it should be noted that, in each case, there were other contributory physiological factors. The testing was subsequently terminated.

(iii) In April 1993, a voluntary physical fitness policy was introduced. The initiative combines physical fitness and a healthy lifestyle. The approach is consistent with the Government's health policy published in the 1992 White Paper "The Health of the Nation" and is linked to the Health Education Council's "Look After Your Heart" workplace project. The voluntary RN PFT is a 1.5 mile time run for the under-40s and a cycle ergometer fitness check for the over-40s. The emphasis is firmly placed on healthy-living education and encouraging voluntary fitness testing; the RN Physical Training Branch plays a major part in the implementation of the programme.

(iv) New Entry Training establishments (BRNC and HMS RALEIGH) and the RN School of Leadership and Management (RNSLAM) conduct mandatory PFTs, and failure to achieve the required standard of physical fitness could contribute to the removal of an individual from a course. BRNC and HMS RALEIGH employ the 1.5 mile run and the Untied States Marine Corps (USMC) test as methods of assessing fitness; standards to be achieved are set out at Annex A. The RNSLAM uses the 1.5 mile run to assess fitness and additional runs of 2, 3 and 5 miles as a team building activity and to improve fitness prior to an exercise in the Black Mountains; these are integral elements of the Leadership Course. The RNSLAM also used the Multistage Fitness Test, a progressive shuttle run, for Petty Officers' Courses; but this has now been replaced by the 1.5 mile run.

(v) The Royal Marines, with a more exacting operational requirement for physical fitness than the RN, have a mandatory test on similar lines to the Army's. Each Royal Marine is required to carry out a Battle Fitness Test every 6 months.

The standard required are at Annex B.

Annexes:

A. PFTs and Standards

B. Royal Marines Battle Fitness Test Standards

ANNEX A

PFTs and Standards

Harvard Step Test

The candidate is required to step up and down from a platform of height 43 cm at a rate of 30 complete steps a minute for 5 minutes. On completion of the exercise, the pulse rate is taken after one, two and three minutes for 30 seconds on each occasion. These are added together and a score of 190 or less is regarded as an indicator of an acceptable level of fitness. This test is still used during diving aptitude tests.

1.5 mile run—1976 Standards

Men

		Under 30	30–34	35–39	40–44	45–49	50–54	55 and over
Times for	1	14.30–12.01	15.00–12.31	15.30–13.01	16.00–13.31	16.30–14.01	17.00–14.31	17.30–15.01
Levels (Minutes	2	12.00–11.01	12.20–11.31	13.00–12.01	13.30–12.06	14.00–12.46	14.30–13.16	15.01–13.45
and	3	11.00–10.16	11.30–10.38	12.00–11.01	12.05–11.16	12.45–11.31	13.15–12.01	13.44–12.31
Seconds)	4	Under 10.16	Under 10.38	Under 11.01	Under 11.16	Under 11.31	Under 12.01	Under 12.31

Level 1 = Poor   Level 3 = Good

Level 2 = Satisfactory Level 4 = Very Good

Women

		Under 30	30–34	35–39	40–44	45–49	50–54	55 and over
Times for	1	17.30–14.31	18.00–15.01	18.30–15.31	19.00–16.01	19.30–16.31	20.00–17.01	20.30–17.31
Levels (Minutes	2	14.30–13.31	15.00–14.01	15.30–14.31	16.00–15.01	16.30–15.31	17.00–16.01	17.30–16.31
and	3	13.30–12.31	14.00–13.01	14.20–13.31	15.00–14.01	15.30–14.31	16.00–15.01	16.30–15.31
Seconds)	4	Under 12.31	Under 13.01	Under 13.31	Under 14.01	Under 14.31	Under 15.01	Under 15.31

1.5 mile run—1993 Standards

	Men	Women
Entry to 28	11 mins	13 mins
29–35	11.5 mins	13.5 mins
36–39	12 mins	14 mins

Multistage Fitness Test

This progressive shuttle-run test is conducted over a flat surface of 20 metres and the participants react to a cassette which starts them all at a very slow pace. The test extends to 21 "levels", each level lasting one minute and changes from one level to the next are indicated by a loud bleep and the recorded voice stating the new level. Each level equates to a VO2 maximum (eg level 14, shuttle 8 would equate to 62.7 ml of oxygen uptake per kilogram of body weight per minute—very good). In the RN, Level 7 (37.1 ml) is considered to be the minimum standard for women and level 10 (47.4 ml) for men.

US Marine Corps Test

Male–Female*

	Poor Sat*	Sat Average*	Average Good*	Good V Good*	V Good Excellent*	Excellent
Sit-ups	25–31	32–38	50–56	67–79	80–85	85+
Press-ups	16–19	20–26	27–30	30–32	33–35	36+
Burpees	17–19	20–22	23–29	30–32	33–35	36+
Shuttle Run (5×60m Grids)	62–60	59–58	57–51	50–49	48–47	45 secs

ANNEX B
ROYAL MARINES BATTLE FITNESS TEST STANDARDS

Under 30: 50 sit-ups
           5 overgrasp pull-ups
           1.5 mile squaded run completed in 15 mins
           1.5 mile run under 11.5 mins

30-34:   40 sit-ups
           4 overgrasp pull-ups
           1.5 mile squaded run completed in 15 mins
           1.5 mile run under 12 mins

35–40:   35 sit-ups
           3 overgrasp pull-ups
           1.5 mile squaded run completed in 15 mins
           1.5 mile run under 13 mins

Over 40:   No sit-ups or pull-ups
           1.5 mile squaded run completed in 15 mins
           1.5 mile run under 15 mins

Results are recorded in Service Documents.

Q7. A note on the RN ships in which CAPES is not deployed (Q361) and the timetable for its introduction, would be helpful.

A7.(i) All SSNs, RFAs and MCM vessels have been fitted with platform models of the Capability Evaluation System (CAPES). Half the DD/FF force has been fitted, with the remainder scheduled to be completed by Autumn 1994.

(ii) CAPES models are being developed for all Fleet Air Arm Squadrons and Flights and it is intended to begin design work for CVSs and LPDs when resources allow. Appropriate models are also being developed for all RM units.

(iii) As soon as the current software is validated in the various platforms, and weighting factors have been adjusted to correspond with current OST and operational standards, it is intended to set CAPES targets for incorporation in the Fleet Management Plan 1995.

Q8. Further to Qq375–6, the Committee has asked for the detailed fuel allocation to flotillas and other comparable units in 1992–93, 1993–94 and the plans for 1994–95.

A8.(i) The Fleet programme is managed within the resources of money and fuel allocated to it. In the allocation of fuel, priority is given to operational tasks and to more important exercises and training. The Surface Flotilla, which comprises all Major Surface Vessels, is the principal user of dieso fuel.

(ii) The actual amount of fuel allocated to the Surface Flotilla in 1992–93 and 1993–94 and the planned allocation for 1994–95 are as follows:

1992–93 – 311,180 cubic metres.

1993–94 – 261,757 cubic metres.

1994–95 – 259,724 cubic metres.

(iii) The above figures exclude the fuel required for operations in the Adriatic, for which exceptional arrangements have been made to ensure that the additional fuel consumed does not affect the provision of fuel for other tasks.

(iv) The allocations, which were derived from the numbers of operational ships and their planned programmes of activity over the period in question, reflect an overall reduction in the numbers of operational Destroyers and Frigates. The allocation for 1993–94 includes an increase of about five per cent over what was originally planned for that year, although it is still lower than the figure for 1992–93. This information supersedes the answer given to Question 376 at the Oral Hearing on 8 December 1993: any confusion is regretted.

Q10. The Committee has asked for details of the recent backlog in naval helicopter training (Qq408, 412) and its operational effects, including any on RN helicopter deployments with UNPROFOR, in the Adriatic, and in Northern Ireland: and a note on the alleged shortfall in submarine availability for ASW training (Q409).

A10.(i) For a variety of reasons there has been a backlog in Naval helicopter training. This has not, however, been allowed to impact on front line operational capability. All commitments have been met in full through careful management of assets and manpower, including those in respect of UNPROFOR and in Northern Ireland.

(ii) One of the causes of the backlog was the loss of RFA ARGUS to other, higher priority operational tasks which placed constraints on embarked pipeline training. When another RFA was available in lieu, some degraded training was possible, although the alteration of embarkation dates exacerbated the backlog by delaying training. On the one occasion when no other RFA was available the training pipeline was stalled.

(iii) Embarked pipeline ASW training makes use of submarines taking part in JMCs. 810 Squadron has been able to take advantage of an increased submarine activity close to RNAS Culdrose because of the use of SSNs for OST and their need to operate in deep water.

(iv) The reduction in the number of submarines within the Fleet has reduced the opportunities for ASW training against real targets. In partial compensation for this, increased use is being made of the Full Mission Simulator ashore and work is in hand to develop and procure submarine simulators and airborne trainers for use at sea. Overall, there are sufficient training opportunities for the frontline ASW Sea King squadrons to maintain a satisfactory level of military capability.

Q11. The Committee wishes to know whether the contract awarded to Dowty-Sema in August 1989 for command systems included any requirement for introductory or advanced skill trainers: whether the CACS 4 programme included funding for development and production of a Combined Tactical Trainer: and when funding for a CTT 5 was agreed (Qq421ff).

A11.(i) The Committee refers to "introductory or advanced skill trainers". There are in fact three levels of Command Systems training: "introductory", which is computer-based familiarisation training at a single console; "intermediate", which introduces individuals to their roles within a Command Team; and "advanced", which is Combined Tactical training within a Command Team simulation. The contract awarded to Dowty-Sema in August 1989 included the provision of the Command System Hardware and Software for use by the Combined Tactical Trainer to provide "advanced" training.

(ii) The initial requirement did not include funding for the development and production of a Combined Tactical Trainer (CTT) as this was to be covered by the existing CACS 1 programme. At the first revise of the Staff Requirement, however, it was considered necessary to include provision for a system for use by a CTT for CACS 4, for which funding was made available.

(iii) Funding for feasibility studies for a CTT 5 was approved in April 1991. The funding requirement for total procurement (including development and production) was also noted at that time; funding approval is normally sought separately for each stage of procurement.

Q12. A note on Sea King availability, as referred to at Q414, would be helpful.

A12.(i) Factors which are reducing availability in the Sea King ASW Fleet are:

(a)   aircraft age and operating environment, leading to increased component and system failure rates;

(b)   timely supply of critical spare parts; and

(c)   a major conversion programme updating the Sea King fleet to ASW Mk 6 standard.

(ii) The financial and manpower burdens of supporting the ASW Sea King are increasing with the age of the aircraft.

(iii) In general, shelf stocks of spares remain sufficient. In some critical areas, however, output from the component repair organisation has not kept pace with demand because of shortages of piece-part spares needed for the repair line.

(iv) Where such shortages have occurred, the Naval Air Command has had to allocate available assets to high priority operational tasks at the expense of training and other commitments.

(v) Several measures are in hand to ensure that an appropriate level of spares is available to support the Sea King. These include the targeting of additional resources, salvage of components within the third-line component repair organisation and increased communication between operators, repair and commodity managers and industry.

8.   Memorandum submitted by the Ministry of Defence answering the Committee's remaining questions on RN training following the oral evidence taken on 8 December 1993 (16 May 1994)

Q5. Further to Qq344ff, the Committee has asked for further explanation of the task book system, if appropriate by example.

A5. THE TASK BOOK SYSTEM

(i) The Task Book System is used by officers and ratings throughout their general and specialist training. For general training, the system is designed to ensure consistency in the training and examination of personnel. The mandatory tasks listed are considered to be the minimum to provide the necessary general naval knowledge and adequate preparation for deeper specialist training at the next stage.

(ii) In the specialist stage, Task Books indicate the training activities which, if they are to be completed satisfactorily, will require on-the-job training, thus providing students with the necessary practical experience to carry out their operational role. The Task Book will also provide instructors with a measure of their students' achievement.

(iii) Several aspects of the Task Book System should be noted:

(a)   they are intended to focus the attention of individuals on their specific role(s) and the wider organisational environment within which the role(s) are performed;

(b)   they impose a self-learning discipline on the individual and set time constraints for the acquisition of those levels of knowledge;

(c)   they provide a system of monitoring to ensure that the required performance standards are met and maintained; and

(d)   they provide a continuous point of reference to aid personal study and revision for examinations and, in the case of ratings, advancement to higher rates.

Q9. Following the exchanges on the move of OST from Portland to Devonport, the Committee has asked for details on progress in re-providing facilities for (a) fixed and rotary wing support; (b) shore accommodation; and (c) naval gunfire, including land bombardment. It has also asked for the proposed timetable for (i) BOST and (ii) COST at Devonport in terms of sea days and harbour days, and the number of blocks in each sea-day; the estimated cost of increased helicopter transfer of staff during sea training at Devonport; a brief description of the manner in which the Portland credit scheme operates, and of any changes to be made to it in the light of the move to Devonport; and a note on the use by FOST of the range facilities associated with the underwater research establishment at Portland.

A9. AVIATION SUPPORT

(a)(i) Fixed wing aviation support to FOST, currently provided by the Fleet Requirements and Direction Unit (FRADU), based at RNAS YEOVILTON, and Flight Refuelling Aviation, based at Hurn, will continue at similar levels following the move to Devonport, albeit with increased transit times to the operating areas. Plans to stage the aircraft through RAF St Mawgan, as a Forward Operating Base (FOB), are under consideration.

(a)(ii) FOST is currently engaged in a FONA-sponsored three months' trial using a Dauphin leased from Bond Helicopters Ltd to evaluate the feasibility of conducting staff transfers (SOOTAX) by civilian aircraft from Plymouth. This is one of the operations being considered to replace the service provided at Portland by 772 Naval Air Squadron and would release valuable Sea King 4 airframes for operational tasks. Ships' Lynx flights will continue to be parented by NAS Portland, and ASW Sea King support will be readily available owing to the proximity of the exercise areas to RNAS Culdrose.

SHORE ACCOMMODATION

(b)(i) Detailed plans for the conversion of Grenville Block, HMS DRAKE, as the headquarters for FOST have been agreed and the contract for building work will be let in early March 1994, with completion planned for the end of the year. Additional accommodation for the large number of Senior Ratings on FOST's staff will be incorporated in the refurbishment of an adjacent building; the Wardroom of HMS DRAKE has the capacity to accept those staff officers who wish to live in.

(b)(ii) Initial indications are that approximately 60 per cent of FOST's staff will live in Service accommodation. There is therefore likely to be no requirement for additional married quarters and no new build has been planned. These estimates will, however, be continually refined as new staff join and any shortfall in existing facilities will be identified.

NAVAL GUNFIRE SUPPORT (NGS)

(c)(i) The only range used by the RN for land bombardment is at Cape Wrath. No land bombardment will take place in the Plymouth areas; this activity will be simulated at sea by firings under the NGS procedures on the proposed Dodman Point range. A MOD Consultative Document is being prepared for a period of direct consultation with Local Authorities, organisations and interested parties.

(c)(ii) Sea Training involves the conduct of anti-air and anti-surface firings as well as NGS. The existing Plymouth sea exercise areas and associated danger areas are currently being reorganised to accommodate the increased activity associated with the arrival of OST. The new areas will be in place by May 1995; they will be permanently activated and when live firings are planned they will be under continuous radar cover to ensure the safety of aircraft which inadvertently stray into areas in which live firings are being conducted. FO Plymouth is responsible for defining these new areas. Existing rights for vessels to transit through and operate in these sea areas will not be affected.

(c)(iii) (1) & (2) *OST Training Packages.*   The Committee asked for the proposed timetable for BOST and COST in terms of sea days and harbour days, and the number of blocks in each sea day. As this question is rather difficult to answer in such terms, it is hoped that the following will provide the information being sought:

(a)   Preliminary Safety Training (2 weeks) is unaltered by the move to Plymouth. It comprises a Staff Sea Check, followed by a harbour training week and one week at sea.

(b)   BOST remains a six weeks' package in Plymouth; the second harbour week (Week 4) will be reduced to three days in order to provide extra time at sea to compensate for increased transit time and the requirement to conduct diving training during the sea weeks because of the pollution levels in Weston Mill Lake.

(c)   COST is in the process of being replaced by DOST (pre-Deployment Operational Sea Training) which is an expansion of the current one week pre-deployment training (PDT) package given to ships deploying on Ministerially Approved Tasks. DOST is a three weeks' package, comprising three days of harbour training followed by 11 sea days, focusing the sea training effort much more clearly than COST on those ships entering the highest readiness categories. It will offer better structured training, at no extra cost and at the ideal time in a ship's programme. This syllabus can be accommodated at Devonport without penalty or additional expense.

(d)   Ships which have recently completed BOST or which are re-deploying within a year of DOST will receive the existing one week PDT in the Plymouth sea areas.

(e)   While the different types of OST exercises vary in length, ships usually conduct three to four "packages" or serial blocks per day and it is planned to conduct broadly similar arrangements in Plymouth, although provision has been made in the BOST package for two extra sea days to allow flexibility in programming and to account for potential constraints on harbour movement.

HELICOPTER TRANSFER COSTS

(d)(i)   Until trial results have been evaluated, an Invitation to Tender issued and bids received, it will not be feasible to make a decision on the precise means by which helicopter support will be provided. It is, therefore, not yet possible to assess the costs of civilian helicopter transfers. It is, however, clear from the early progress of the current trial that, both in terms of speed of transfer and airframe availability, a commercial aircraft is more efficient than the existing arrangements which rely on Sea King Mk 4 helicopters.

(d)(ii)   The balance between helicopter SOOTAX and boat transfers in Plymouth will depend upon the numbers and types of ships undergoing OST at a given time, weather conditions and the requirements of other users of Plymouth Sound.

PORTLAND CREDIT SCHEME

(e)(i)   For many years, FOST has made use of diesel electric submarines (SSK) from other NATO nations to assist in providing ASW training to ships undergoing OST. The Portland Credit Scheme (PCS) allows the cost of such submarine time to be offset against provision of OST to surface ships from the nations concerned (Germany and the Netherlands). Data are routinely gathered on the staff cover and external assets provided to NATO ships, and these are converted to attributable costs based on rates set annually by the MOD. Similarly, the ASW exercise hours contributed by each submarine are recorded and corresponding costs assessed.

(e)(ii)   An expanded note on the operation of the Portland Credit Scheme is at Annex A.

RANGE USAGE

(f)   FOST makes no direct use of the noise and magnetic signature range facilities associated with the activities of the Directorate of Test and Evaluation (Sea Systems) although, as convenient to their pre-OST programmes, some ships conduct routine noise ranging during their shakedown training.

ANNEX A

THE PORTLAND CREDIT SCHEME

(i)   The Portland Credit Scheme (PCS) is an agreement dating back to 1976 between the UK, the Federal German Navy (FGN) and the Royal Netherlands Navy (RNLN) under which FGN and RNLN vessels undertake Operational Sea Training (OST) at Portland and offset the repayment costs by the provision, to an equivalent cash value, of submarine time and staff time in support of OSTs. No actual cash changes hands but the value of the receipts forgone in terms of the provision of OST and the value to the UK in terms of the submarine time provided are monitored and recorded on the appropriate account.

(ii)   The arrangements for the PCS are subject to detailed accounting procedures in order to maintain a broad balance between the participating countries. Inevitably, the requirements for OST and submarine time vary from one year to another. There is therefore provision under the scheme to use credit built up in one year to offset against the need in another. Any party to the Agreement could call in the cash balance of transactions at any time and, although this is unlikely, it means that there is a technical need to record any potential liability through a proper account.

(iii) Each month a statement is produced detailing the amount of time in hours and specific resources consumed in providing training to the FGN and RNLN, together with a statement of the amount of FGN submarine time and RNLN submarine and staff time provided in support of OST. This information is costed, according to the latest schedule of charges and brought to account on the relevant expenditure and receipt internal account codes (IACs). The schedule of charges is established using standard Departmental policy for repayment together with an assessment of the hourly cost to the UK of the use of a conventional submarine. Each participating nation is informed annually of the state of the account with them so that plans can be developed for the coming year for the level of participation.

(iv) As no actual cash changes hands, it is necessary to balance the transactions within the overall reconciliation with the appropriation account. Towards the end of the financial year a decision is taken on the timing of the final bookings so that an accrual transaction can be inserted into the ledger which results from the net balance between the "income" and "expenditure". This reconciles the cash accounts and is recognised as a potential liability carried forward into the following year.

(v) An indication of the scale of the PCS is given by figures for the year 1992/93: at the start of the year, the UK was owed services from the FGN and RNLN worth £77,000; during the year they provided to the UK £1.1 million worth of submarine and staff time to set against their requirements for training from the UK valued at £0.656 million; consequently, at the end of the year the UK owed training to the FGN and RNLN worth £0.367 million.

(vi) No change is expected to the PCS (other than to its name) as a result of the move to Devonport.

Q13. The Committee also sought copies of:

(a) the Layard Study (Qq290-1);

(b) the Investment Appraisal on Manadon (Qq336-7);

(c) the "Fleet charge" paper referred to at Q368;

(d) the Plymouth University Report referred to (Q384); and

(e) the Investment Appraisal of the decision to establish a new Cookery Training School at HMS Raleigh, and RN Cook drop-out figures at Aldershot (Qq417ff).

A13(a)(i) Attached is a synopsis of the report of the Officers' Study Group*.

(ii) Development work to carry forward around a hundred recommendations of the Officers' Study Group is well under way with the aim of making progressive further reports to the Navy Board between now and the early part of next year. Implementation of some recommendations has begun (for example, raising the Admiralty Interview Board pass mark to 500) and further aspects can be expected to be implemented during 1995. For new entrants, a significant package of new terms of service is planned for introduction on 1 April 1996. Careful consideration will be given to the transitional arrangements needed to ensure that currently serving officers are not unfairly treated during the change to a new structure for the officer corps. Development work will have to be conducted in parallel with the independent review of Service career and manpower structures and terms and conditions of service which was announced in January. Similarly, proposals stemming from the current Defence Costs Study will have to be taken into account.

(iii) The Committee may wish to note that a study of the Rating Corps is about to begin, and here too account will need to be taken of the independent review.

(b)(i) The proposal to cease first degree education for RN Engineer Officers at the Royal Naval Engineering College at Manadon, Plymouth, was outlined in the Consultative Document "Tri-Service Support Rationalisation—Engineer Officer Training" issued on 25 May 1993. The Minister for the Armed Forces confirmed the proposal on 16 September 1993, and subsequent work has been devoted to the future of the remaining training activities at Manadon and of the site itself.

(ii) It was recognised in the Consultative Document that a possible consequence of removing first degree education from Manadon might well be that it would be difficult to justify the continued retention of the site by the Ministry of Defence unless alternative Defence activities could be transferred there. Since then, the Ministry has conducted a significant amount of work with the aim of either identifying alternative Defence activities that could possibly be transferred to the site or transferring Manadon's remaining activities to other RN training establishments. The options that have emerged from this work have now been subjected to Investment Appraisal (IA) and the conclusions drawn are set out in the paragraphs below.

(iii) The largest residual training activity remaining at Manadon is Systems Engineering and Management Training (SEMT), formerly known as Application Training. This is post-degree training aimed at familiarising Engineer Officer graduates with the actual technological systems encountered in the Marine, Weapon and Aeronautical Engineering specialisms. The IA therefore examined a number of options, including, on the one hand, the retention of SEMT at Manadon (with or without the transfer in of other training activities to use spare

*Not printed.

capacity) and, on the other, the transfer of SEMT to alternative RN training establishments, namely HMS SULTAN and HMS COLLINGWOOD. Of those options, the IA examined in detail and costed the following:

Option 0—Retain SEMT at Manadon along with residual functions.

Option 1—Move SEMT to HMS SULTAN and HMS COLLINGWOOD and dispose of the Manadon site.

Option 2—Move Britannia Royal Naval College New Entry Training to Manadon alongside SEMT.

Option 3—Move Air Engineering School (AES) from HMS DAEDALUS to Manadon alongside SEMT.

(iv) Two variants of Option 3 were also considered, namely:

(a) moving the Department of Nuclear Science and Technology from the Royal Naval College Greenwich to Manadon with the AES; and

(b) moving to RN Hydrographic School from HMS DRAKE to Manadon.

Neither move, however, would result in the total vacation of the parent establishment. The result would be that not only would Manadon be under-used but so also would be Greenwich and/or HMS DRAKE. Moreover, it would be impossible to achieve, in anything like an acceptable timescale, savings of the order required to offset the high relocation costs. These variants of Option 3 were therefore discounted at an early stage.

(v) The attached costing tables* show that, at average 1993–94 prices and in terms of Net Present Value over twenty years:

(a) Option 0 costs £105 million. It is against this baseline that the other options have been costed;

(b) Option 1 has early works and relocation costs of almost £12 million but would yield a saving of over £40 million; and

(c) Option 2 would yield a saving of £25 million; whereas

(d) Option 3 would cost more than Option 0.

(vi) The IA concluded that Option 1—to relocate SEMT to HMS SULTAN and HMS COLLINGWOOD with the consequential disposal of the Manadon site—is the most cost-effective option, and that this outcome is robust in the face of risk and sensitivity analysis.

(vii) The usual Redundant Lands and Accommodation (RLA) procedure to establish other single-Service or wider MOD interest in the site has been undertaken. These enquiries have not resulted in any firm proposal and are unlikely to do so.

(viii) The combined staff implications of the discontinuation of in-Service first degree education and, now, the proposal to vacate RNEC Manadon altogether will, as foreshadowed in the May 1993 Consultative Document, affect a total of some 175 staff, of whom about 75 are mobile and 100 are non-mobile. Every attempt will be made to find alternative employment in MOD or in other Government Departments for all the staff affected, but the scale of the combined effects of these proposals will mean that compulsory redundancies may be inevitable. Any staff made redundant will be compensated under the terms of the Principal Civil Service Pension Scheme or the appropriate staff regulations. In addition, all staff made redundant will have access to the MOD Outplacement Service (MODOPS) to assist them in identifying new opportunities. The MOD will also be in contact with the Department of Employment and the local Training and Enterprise Councils (TECs).

(ix) The plans for the future conduct of all Engineer Officer Training described above are consistent with the Navy Board's policy of rationalising the RN's training infrastructure and the concentration of activities at "core" establishments, which include HMS SULTAN and HMS COLLINGWOOD. Account has also been taken of other current work which could result in further changes in the way in which naval training is planned and delivered and it has been concluded that the most cost-effective course is for SEMT to be transferred to the Portsmouth area, with other minor training activities being also transferred away from Manadon. Consequently, the Royal Navy will cease to require the site by 1996 and will therefore, subject to the receipt of views following the consultation process, take the necessary action with the Defence Lands Services to dispose of the site.

(c) As requested, a copy of Fleet Charge Document 3, which covers the maintenance of military capability within the Fleet, is attached.*

(d) (i) A copy of the University of Plymouth report on "The Integration of Sea Service" is attached.*

(ii) Although originally classified RESTRICTED, it has now been declassified. The University of Plymouth have however expressly asked that the report should not be published because of a correlation with work that the University is seeking to undertake in other quarters concerning the wider employment of women.

(e) (i) The following paragraphs outline the rationale, in both managerial and financial terms, behind the decision to transfer the RN Cookery School from St Omer Barracks, Aldershot, to HMS RALEIGH in Cornwall.

*Not printed.

BACKGROUND

(ii) The RN Cookery School was originally located in HMS PEMBROKE, Chatham. Following a tri-Service study into catering training (at about the time of the demise of Chatham Dockyard), a decision was taken to concentrate it at St Omer Barracks, Aldershot, the aim being to create a tri-Service cookery school. The RN Cookery School therefore moved to Aldershot in September 1983.

(iii) The majority of the savings envisaged as a consequence of the move to Aldershot were dependent upon merging the three single-Service schools. These savings have since proved impossible to realise because of the differing nature of the training required by each of the Services. St Omer Barracks therefore remains merely a home for three collocated schools rather than one combined school.

THE PROBLEMS

(iv) Despite ongoing attempts to achieve satisfactory training arrangements at Aldershot, significant problems remain:

(a)   the training and living accommodation arrangements for RN personnel are far from ideal;

(b)   there are significant man management problems generated by separation of the trainees from the RN environment with which they are familiar. These are reflected in the drop-out rates about which the Committee has asked and on which a note is at Annex A;

(c)   the Cookery School is separated from its parent organisation, the RN Supply School at HMS RALEIGH; and

(d)   the kitchens at Aldershot required major and costly refurbishment to enable them to comply with the Food Safety Act 1990.

THE WAY FORWARD

(v) In order to overcome these problems, three main options were considered:

(a)   do nothing;

(b)   remain at St Omer Barracks, making changes to improve the RN's position; and

(c)   relocate the RN Cookery School to HMS RALEIGH.

No other geographical locations were considered because it was foreseen that, if savings—especially in staff costs—were to result from a move away from Aldershot, they were unlikely to be achieved other than by absorbing the task into the RN Supply School at HMS RALEIGH. The "do nothing" option was untenable, not least because of the demands of the Food Safety Act. Thus, the options were reduced to two, both of which necessitated considerable capital expenditure. The cash flows (at average 1992–93 prices) on works services, equipment, staffing costs, travel and subsistence were assessed to have the following Net Present Values (excluding VAT):

remain at St Omer Barracks — £9.9 million;

move to HMS RALEIGH   — £8.8 million.

(vi) Apart from the financial arguments for relocation to HMS RALEIGH, the savings from which are acknowledged as being modest, non-financial considerations played an important part in the decision. The principal non-financial factors were those at sub-paragraphs (iv)(a) and (iv)(b) above, including the high training wastage rate at Aldershot. The conclusion was reached that no time should be lost in pressing ahead with the move to HMS RALEIGH.

THE PRESENT POSITION

(vii) In consideration of the most economical method of accommodating the School at HMS RALEIGH, three realistic options presented themselves:

(a)   a new build to the south of HMS RALEIGH's Trafalgar Galley;

(b)   a single-storey link to Trafalgar Galley; and

(c)   a new build to the north of Trafalgar Galley.

The first of these options was chosen; not only was it the cheapest, but the other two had unacceptable risks associated with them, mainly in respect of ventilation, other Health and Safety Act considerations, accessibility and the nature of the terrain. * * * * (including fees and VAT) at average 1992–93 prices. The contract for the new build was let in January 1994 and the work is expected to be finished in the autumn of this year.

ANNEX B

RN Cook Drop-Out Rates at St Omer Barracks, Aldershot

1. The RN cook drop-out rates for the three years to 31 March 1993 were:

	Male	*Female*
1990–91	47%	14%
1991–92	58%	52%
1992–93	32%	25%

2. The principal reasons for such significant drop-out rates are considered to be:

(a)   the absence of a RN corporate identity in an Army environment;

(b)   the culture clash between RN ratings and Army other ranks; and

(c)   to some, the relative unattractiveness of the trade itself.

3. It is expected that the above drop-out rates will be significantly reduced when the RN Cookery Training School is established at HMS RALEIGH in 1994–95.

9.   Memorandum submitted by the Ministry of Defence answering the Committee's questions on RAF training (4 February 1994)

Q1. A note on the TLB, HLB and IHLB structure and expenditure as it applies to RAF training would be helpful, together with details of progress towards Defence Agency status.

BUDGETARY STRUCTURE

A1(i)   The Training Group (TG) is a Higher Level Budget (HLB) within the RAF Support Command (RAFSC) Top Level Budget (TLB). It comprises 13 Basic Level Budgets (BLB) and six non-BLB units together with the Air Officer Commanding's (AOC) Headquarters staff. The RAFSC TLB contains separate HLBs for the training conducted at RAF College Cranwell and RAF Staff College Bracknell. The TG's budgetary structure will not change when the TG becomes an integral part of RAF Personnel & Training Command (PTC) on 1 April 1994.

(ii)   The diagram at Annex A shows the planned PTC budgetary structure.

EXPENDITURE

(iii)   The TG's cash budget in FY93/94 is £312 million. This figure includes expenditure on salaries, contracts and ancillary running costs; it also includes the cost of the Group's parenting responsibilities for lodger units of other Commands.

DEFENCE AGENCY

(iv)   A comprehensive programme of action is underway to ensure the successful launch of the TG Defence Agency (TGDA) on 1 April 1994. The AOC will be the Agency's Chief Executive.

(v)   The TGDA's corporate documentation has been produced on schedule and will be presented as part of the formal Ministerial endorsement process which is due to begin around the end of January 1994. The documentation includes the Agency's key targets for its first year of operation. The Agency's Framework Document has been passed to the Trades Union side in accordance with standard consultation procedures.

(vi)   The TGDA's corporate planning process has identified a number of strategic directions including improved resource management and business development which will allow it to manage its business more cost-effectively. To achieve these strategic aims the Agency is preparing its case for the additional freedoms and delegations it requires. These will be embodied in formal letters of delegation to be issued to the Chief Executive at the time of launch.

(vii)   The National Audit Office has carried out a review of the TG's accounting systems and policies. The recommendations made in the subsequent report are being used to develop the Group's financial regime, which will be supported by a Financial & Management Accounting System. In order to produce the Agency's opening balances, the Group's fixed assets are in the process of being valued by the Defence Lands Service and the Valuation Office Agency.

(viii)   Preparation of the TG for Defence Agency status has been undertaken in conjunction with the Department's Next Steps Framework Team and officials from the Central Departments.

Q2. It would be helpful to have table showing the numbers in the various relevant categories entering and leaving the training system each year since 1990, and anticipated future levels from 1995–96.

FLYING TRAINING

A2(i)   The numbers in the various relevant categories entering and leaving flying training each year since 1990 are shown at Annex B. The anticipated future levels for 1995–96 and for the steady state are at Annex C. It must be appreciated that the Into Training Target (ITT) numbers and the Into Productive Service (IPS) figures in any year do not bear any relation to each other, as the training cycle takes from 2 to 3 years depending on category.

GROUND TRAINING

(ii) Definitions of the various types of ground training undertaken by the TG are at Annex D. The statistics for planned intakes for the period FY93/94 to 03/04 are at Annex E, and the statistics for actual intake/outflow numbers for FY90/91 to 92/93 are at Annex F.

Q3. A note on the outcome to date of any mark testing of RAF training, and of future plans, would be helpful.

ACHIEVEMENT TO DATE

A3(i) The Group has been in the vanguard of the application of market testing principles to military training. The summary at Annex G shows the results since 1988 together with the range and value of activities that have been contractorised. The value of the contracts is commercially confidential. Significantly, elementary flying training and the engineering and supply functions at the majority of the flying training stations are now performed by contractors.

(ii) A total of 2,482 posts have been saved since 1988; the value of current contracts during FY93/94 is £30.80 million.

PROGRAMME TO 31 MARCH 1996

(iii) In the period 1 April 1992 to 31 March 1996 the Training Group proposes to market test some £45.6 million of business. Future measures will be the subject of consultation as they are announced.

PROGRAMME AFTER 1 APRIL 1996

(iv) Work is well advanced in developing a strategy for market testing future areas of the Group's activities after 1 April 1996. The work is being done in concert with the overarching strategy for the future application of market testing principles to the RAF's business that is being developed.

(v) The Defence Agency intends to employ market testing as a key to greater efficiency in training.

Q4. It would be helpful to have a note setting out the principal changes in RAF pilot selection and training since the memorandum provided for the Committee in April 1980, including changes in the aircraft used and in the bases used for training.

A4(i) There have been two significant changes to pilot selection since 1980: the introduction of computer-based testing, and the introduction of the P-score.

(ii) In 1981 the HCDC recommended that "Computer-based equipment should be introduced in an effort to improve the prediction of success in training". Since then, the three tests in the 1950s pilot aptitude tests used in the early 1980s have been replaced with five validated computer-based tests which together give a broader basis for measurement and enhanced predictability for Basic Flying Training (BFT). In addition, the two 1950s navigator tests have also been replaced by five computer-based tests. It is fair to say that the current computer-based tests have generated worldwide interest, and indeed are being used under licence by many air forces and airlines. Nonetheless, while computer-based testing has been in place since 1985, the fully revised battery of tests has only been extant for about a year. Over the period 1985–92 the computerised tests were fully validated against success at BFT.

(iii) The second major change in testing policy was the introduction of a Probability Score (P-Score). A report in 1983, showed that by an optimum combination of the most significant measures recorded at OASC (personal characteristics, attainments and aptitude), a P-score could be calculated for each candidate giving his/her chance of success at BFT. P-score was introduced at OASC in 1983 and has been used ever since. The concept was re-validated and the formula adjusted during the last 5 years.

(iv) The main changes in pilot training are covered in the sequence of training stages.

(a) *Elementary Flying Training (EFT).* EFT was introduced in 1985 as a 64 hour course on the Chipmunk aircraft for those entering the RAF with less than 30 hours previous flying experience (PFE). The aim of the course was to produce a pilot of equivalent standard to the University Air Squadron graduate who could cope with the Short Basic Flying Training (BFT) course of 92 hours. Wastage rates for EFT graduates proved broadly comparable to those of UAS graduates, and considerably less than those with more than 30 hours PFE, who completed the Long BFT course (109 hours). We hope that it can be proved cost-effective to provide EFT for all non-UAS students and make the BFT short course standard for all—with consequent savings in Tucano flying. In 1991 the EFT course was refined to 53 hours, and in 1992 the RN and RAF EFTSs combined to form the Joint Elementary Flying Training Squadron (JEFTS), a fully contractorised unit (including most of the flying instruction) operated by Hunting Aviation using the Slingsby Firefly light propeller-driven aircraft.

(b) *Basic Flying Training (BFT).* The major changes in BFT since 1980 have been the closure in 1992 of the BFTS at RAF Church Fenton, because of reduced requirement, and the replacement of the Jet Provost aircraft by the Tucano. The Tucano is much cheaper to operate, has tandem seating like the Hawk, and is supported by excellent synthetic training aids including full motion simulators and computer-based training packages. The last Jet Provost course finished in June 1993.

(c) *Fast-Jet Advanced Flying Training (FJAFT).* In 1992 a 100 hour Hawk course was introduced combining the former AFT and Tactical Weapons courses with consequent savings; this enabled the closure of RAF Brawdy, and RAF Chivenor was transferred to RAF Support Command so that the new course could be run in parallel at Valley and Chivenor. After the 100 hour course pilots go direct to the fast-jet operational conversion units (OCUs). A proposal to place RAF Chivenor in care and maintenance was recently announced. From October 1994 all Hawk pilot training would be concentrated at RAF Valley. A final decision will be announced shortly.

(d) *Multi-engine Advanced Flying Training.* No change; the Jetstream remains in service in this role.

(e) *Helicopter Advanced Flying Training.* The introduction of navigators into support helicopters in 1992 led to the adoption of the concept of conjoint training in which pilot, navigator and crewman join the same course, often flying together to maximise the training value of each sortie. The new cost-effective syllabus is flown sequentially on the Gazelle and the Wessex.

Q5. It would be helpful to have a progress report on the proposals for reorganisation announced on 6 November 1992, including on any disposal of land as a result.

A5(i) The Ground Training Rationalisation (GTR) project was announced on 6 November 1992 with the aim of initially reducing the ground training estate from 6 to 3 sites; RAF Cosford (Technical Training), RAF Halton (Administrative Training) and RAF Locking (Telecommunications Training). A further study was to be carried out into the rationalisation of RAF Locking.

(ii) *School of Recruit Training.* Recruit training was transferred from RAF Swinderby to RAF Halton in 1993. The 17 December 1993 target date for closing RAF Swinderby was met and the station was handed to Defence Lands Services (DLS) for disposal. A disposal strategy is being formulated.

(iii) *RAF Hereford.* The transfer of the Airman's Command School to RAF Halton was achieved on target in January 1994. The Secretarial and Supply training schools will transfer to RAF Halton in July 1994. RAF Hereford will be offered for disposal in December 1994.

(iv) *RAF Cosford.* The transfer of technical training from RAF Halton started in August 1993 with the movement of propulsion training. Further moves are dependent on the completion of building works for domestic and functional accommodation.

(v) *RAF Newton.* The plan to move the RAF Police School, the Training Development and Support Unit and the Management Training Wing to RAF Halton is progressing. The units are due to move in early 1995; actual dates are dependent on the completion of works services at RAF Cosford and RAF Halton.

(vi) *RAF Locking.* A further study into the possible rationalisation of RAF Locking is currently being carried out.

ANNEX A

PTC Budgetary Structure—Training HLBs

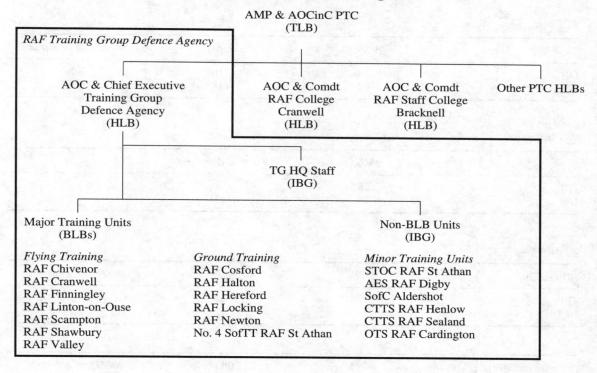

ANNEX B

Aircrew Categories Entering and Leaving Training Since 1990

1. RAF aircrew into training by FY 90/91-92/93

FY	Pilots	Navs	Airmen aircrew
90/91	305	102	81
91/92	165	51	78
92/93	136	51	17
Total	606	204	176

Note:
These figures include students who have changed from ground branches to air branches.

2. RAF aircrew into productive service (IPS) Fy 90/91-92/93

FY	Pilots	Navs	Airmen aircrew
90/91	167	85	73
91/92	127	49	56
92/93	104	51	55
Total	398	185	184

3. Planned ITT and IPS figures for FY 93/94

FY	Pilots	Navs	Airmen aircrew
ITT	75	32	29
IPS	87	34	57

ANNEX C

Anticipated Future Levels of Aircrew Training

1. Pilots

	94/95	95/96	96/97 and onwards
ITT	70	116	208
IPS	93	118	140

2. Navigators

	94/95	95/96 and onwards
ITT	58	59
IPS	44	45

3. Airmen aircrew

(a) AEOp

	94/95	95/96	98/99 and onwards
ITT	13	14	30
IPS	15	12	26

(b) Air Engineers

	94/95	95/96	98/99 and onwards
ITT	6	6	8 [1]
IPS	6	6	8

(c) ALM

	94/95	95/96	98/99 and onwards
ITT	16	20	33
IPS	16	19	30 [2]

Notes:
(1) Will depend on the Hercules replacement.
(2) Will depend on the new Medium Support Helicopter (unlikely to decrease; could increase).

ANNEX D

Definitions of Training

Recruit Training	General service training to accustom airmen/women recruits to service life and to develop a sense of pride and responsibility to the service.
Initial Officer Training	Recruit training for prospective officers.
Initial Specialist Training	Officer Initial Professional Training, e.g. for Engineering, Supply, Secretarial branches.
Basic Trade Training	Airmen/women initial trade training for specific trades, e.g. Airframe mechanic, MT mechanic, Personnel administrator, Supplier, etc.
Further Training	To expand basic trade knowledge for skills not acquired by experience; normally leads to promotion.
Pre-Employment Training	To enable personnel to qualify for employment on specific complex equipment or duties for which training was not covered on Basic or Further Training.
Other Training	e.g., Refresher (Update training) and Assimilation (training required as result of trade group re-organisation).

ANNEX E

RAFSC Ground Training: Planned intakes for FY 93/94 to 03/04

NP/FY	Recruit	Initial	Basic	Further	Pet	Other	Total
93							
93/94	699	2,679	938	5,744	20,837	3,248	33,545
94	810						
95	2,000						
96	4,200						
97	3,500						
98	5,000						
99	5,750						
00	5,750						
01	5,750						
02	5,750						
03	5,300						

Notes:

1. Planned intake figures for all elements of ground training only available for FY 93/94. Thereafter, planned intake figures only currently available for recruit training.

2. Information source — D/Air Sec/26/1/4/2/94 dated 5 October 1993 and Ground Training Stats.

ANNEX F

RAFSC Ground Training: Actual intake/outflow numbers for FYs 90/91 to 92/93

MP/FY	Recruit (Airmen/women)		Initial Training and Initial Specialist Training (for Officers)		Basic Trade Training (Airmen/women)		Further Training (Airmen/women)		Pre-employment Training (Officers and Airmen/women)		Other Types of Training (for Officers and Airmen/women)		Total	
	Intake	Outflow	Intake	Outflow	Intake	Outflow	Intake	Outflow	Intake	Outflow	Intake	Outflow	Intake	Outflow
90														
90/91	5,858	6,153	3,284	3,208	5,977	6,151	7,356	7,851	11,942	12,080	2,797	2,876	37,214	38,319
91														
91/92	3,421	3,936	2,607	2,736	3,980	4,906	5,307	5,586	13,569	13,251	3,194	3,179	32,078	33,594
92														
92/93	792	989	2,189	2,053	1,256	2,676	4,565	4,409	14,766	14,783	2,841	2,697	26,409	27,607

Note:

Information source — RAFSC Progress Return of Adult Ground Training (RAF Stats 254).

ANNEX G

Training Group Market Testing Programme
Summary of Achievement against RAF Market Testing Working Group Action Plan
(Measures stem from action put in hand by AMSO Contractorisation Steering Group)

Station/Unit	Contract	Let/Relet	FY93/94 Value of Contracts	Posts saved at time contract 1st let Service	Civilian
Church Fenton[1]	Multi-activity[2]	88/89	****	238	16
Swinderby[1]	Multi-activity[2]	88/89	****	92	22
Cranwell	Multi-activity[2]	89/90	****	342	42
Linton-on-Ouse	Multi-activity[2]	89/90	****	317	16
Finningley	Multi-activity[2]	91/92	****	664	34
Shawbury	Multi-activity[2]	91/92	****	280	39
Swinderby[1][3]	Catering	91/92	****	—[4]	—[4]
				1,933	169
Scampton[5][6]	Multi-activity	Apr 93	****	324	24
Topcliffe[6]	Elementary Flying	Jul 93	****	32	0
Total			£30.80m	2,289	193

Notes:

1. Station now closed.
2. Original contracts covered Eng. & Supply only; relet contracts include domestic support.
3. Contract covered food preparation and service only.
4. Re-let of long-standing contract; savings NK.
5. Excludes Red Arrows, TMTS and Tornado Radar Repair Unit.
6. Counted against DP92 achievement.

10. Memorandum submitted by the Ministry of Defence answering the Committee's questions following the oral evidence taken on 23 March 1994 (13 May 1994)

Q1. The Committee was offered notes on the instructor system, with numbers, location, rank etc (Q1334); and on comparative flying hours (Q1372). It would be helpful to have full details of the physical fitness tests (Q1371); of the CCS programme (Q1354); and of basic recruit training for airmen and women in military skills, including specification as to the numbers and proportions required to be trained in the use of personal weapons (Q1354).

A1. *The Instructor System*

Qualified Flying Instructors (QFI) are graded according to qualification and experience:

B2—Newly qualified probationary instructor.
B1—Minimum 6 months instructing and 120 instructional hours (including 5 hours night).
A2—Minimum 15 months instructing and 250 instructional hours (including 10 hours night).
A1—Minimum 24 months instructing and 400 instructional hours.

The aim is for all senior supervisors to be at least grade A2, with not more than one-third of instructors at any establishment being grade B2. Exam Wing (Central Flying School) validate flying standards across the RAF.

NUMBERS, LOCATION AND RANK

The numbers, locations and ranks of RAF Flying Instructors for each aircraft role are as follows:

(a) *Elementary Flying Training* (EFT) is conducted at the Joint Elementary Flying Training Squadron at Topcliffe, Yorkshire, using the Slingsby T 67 Firefly. There are 17 Civilian FI's, plus 1 RAF and 4 RN QFI.

(b) *Basic Flying Training* (BFT) is conducted by 1 FTS at Linton-on-Ouse and 3 FTS at Cranwell using the Tucano. There are 3 Squadron Leaders (Sqn Ldr) and 35 Flight Lieutenants (Flt Lt) at Linton, and 3 Sqn Ldr and 36 Flt Lt at Cranwell.

(c) *Fast Jet Advanced Flying Training* (FJAFT) is presently conducted by 4 FTS at Valley and 7 FTS at Chivenor, using the Hawk. There are 2 Sqn Ldr and 32 Flt Lt at each location. (Post 1 April 1995 training will be rationalised at Valley, where the Instructor complement will be 2 Sqn Ldr and 56 Flt Lt.)

(d) *Rotary Wing Advanced Flying Training* (RWAFT) is conducted by 2 FTS at Shawbury, using Gazelle and Wessex helicopters. There are 2 Sqn Ldr and 27 Flt Lt.

(e) *Multi-Engine Advanced Flying Training* (MEAFT) is conducted by 6 FTS at Finningley, using the BAe Jetstream. There is 1 Sqn Ldr and 13 Flt Lt.

COMPARATIVE FLYING HOURS

The following Table compares RAF flying and simulator hours with those flown by the French Air Force (FAF), United States Air Force (USAF), and the Euro Nato Joint Jet Pilot Training (ENJJPT) programme which is used by 11 other NATO countries:

	RAF *Flying/Sim*	FAF *Flying/Sim*	USAF *Flying/Sim*	ENJJPT *Flying/Sim*
EFT	54/–	(1) 10/–	21/–	–/–
BFT	130/28	138/34 (2)	89/27	260/–
FJAFT/	100/32	85/30	119/28	
ATTU		55/12	18/–	(3)
TOTAL	284/60	288/76	247/55	260/–

Notes: (1) Flying grading only.
(2) Uses a static simulator.
(3) A follow-on Advanced Tactical Training Unit (ATTU) course of 18 hours has been introduced pre Operational Conversion Unit; only the US, German and Norwegian students participate.

COMPARISON OF SYLLABUS CONTENT

RAF and FAF

Total flying hours are broadly the same, but the FAF fly more hours on the more expensive Alpha Jet.

RAF and USAF/ENJJPT

USAF and ENJJPT Flying Training (FT) philosophy differs markedly from that of the RAF; it is pre-planned and largely inflexible. The US FT syllabus places greater emphasis on procedural instrument flying and formation flying, but excludes a number of elements which are taught at RAF Basic Flying Training School (BFTS), for example low level navigation to 250ft, free navigation and no-notice diversion techniques, practice forced landings and glide landings.

PHYSICAL FITNESS TEST

Details of the RAF Physical Fitness Test, by age group, is as follows:

(a) *Personnel aged 17–39 years* undertake an aerobic test and two muscular endurance tests. The aerobic test is a multi-stage fitness test which involves running a series of 20 metre shuttles, at an increasing tempo, until the RAF standard is achieved or the individual can no longer maintain the pace. The muscular endurance tests consist of sit-ups and press-ups, which females undertake against a beam or bar set at a height of 60cm.

(b) *Personnel aged 40–49 years,* and older volunteers, complete a sub-maximal aerobic test and a simple test of grip strength. The aerobic test involves pedalling a cycle ergometer against increasing resistance until the monitored heart rate reaches a steady state of 130–150 beats per minute. The grip test involves squeezing a hand-grip dynamometer to record strength in both hands.

(c) *Personnel aged 50+* are not required to undertake a physical fitness test, but may do so voluntarily.

CCS PROGRAMME

The need for a Common Core Skills (CCS) concept was identified in the 1988–90 Review of Ground Defence Training (GDT). The overall objectives were to standardise the training of those elements of GDT which were common throughout the RAF; to reduce the time tradesmen were diverted from their primary tasks to attend annual GDT training; and to reduce the number of RAF Regiment GDT Instructors.

In contrast to the previous requirement of individuals to simply attend mandatory annual GDT training, the emphasis of CCS is on an annual objective test of retained skills and knowledge in four "core" competencies: Surviving Enemy Ground Attack, First Aid, Surviving Air and NBC Attacks, and Post-Attack Recovery Measures. The aim is to achieve an 85 per cent first time pass rate in these essential war-fighting and basic survival skills, in lieu of the two or more days undertaken on GDT previously by all ranks. RAF personnel have each been issued with an aide memoir which contains all the information required to achieve a satisfactory pass. Those who fail in any one of the four "core" areas are required to undertake remedial training.

Upon introduction, CCS failed to deliver the desired first time pass rate, the greatest areas of difficulty being those requiring manipulative skills. However, results are steadily improving. RAF Station Management Plans now indicate an 80 per cent or higher success rate in CCS, with results from those with no previous GDT being particularly encouraging. To maintain the momentum of progress, work is in hand to evaluate the possibility of introducing video and computer based training, and inter-active remedial self-teaching packages. This would reduce still further the diversion of personnel from their primary duties, as well as the number of GDT Instructors required.

It is worthy of note that the RAF CCS programme has been adopted as the tri-Service standard of common military training in both the Falkland Isles and Gibraltar.

BASIC RECRUIT TRAINING

Airmen and women entrants to the RAF, other than RAF Regiment Gunners, undergo seven weeks of recruit training at RAF Halton, Buckinghamshire. The course covers basic military skills and knowledge and is designed to prepare recruits for the next, more specialist, stage of their career training. The following topics are addressed:

(a) *General Service Knowledge (GSK)*. GSK provides recruits with information on Service procedures, regulations and customs, sufficient to deal with problems and events which are likely to arise during this formative stage of their career. The topics covered include: discipline, security, welfare, equipment and clothing, career structure, and the History of the RAF.

(b) *General Service Training (GST)*. GST teaches recruits the practical skills of looking after themselves, their clothing and equipment.

(c) *Drill and Ceremonial.* This covers the basic elements of foot drill and arms drill. It culminates in a passing out parade.

(d) *Ground Defence Training (GDT)*. GDT provides training in the rules of engagement, field-craft, Nuclear, Biological and Chemical Defence, first aid, post attack recovery, fire fighting, and the use of personal weapons by all entrants.

(e) *Physical Education (PE)*. PE is provided to ensure recruits attain an acceptable level of physical fitness required to complete recruit training.

(f) *Padres Hours.* Padres hours gives the recruit the opportunity to learn about the role of Chaplains in the RAF, and to participate in Christian worship. it also gives them the opportunity to discuss more personal matters, such as relationships, personal values and alcohol abuse.

Excluding RAF Regiment Gunners, the number of recruits trained during the last three Financial Years (FY) was as follows:

FY 91–92	FY 92–93	FY 93–94
3,333	886	588

THE RAF REGIMENT GUNNERS

To minimise overlap and total training time, basic recruit training and specialist training for RAF Regiment Gunners is delivered as a single course. Because of the nature of their role, Gunners receive more intensive training in many military skills, including the use of personal weapons.

Q2. Further to Q1356, and to the comments at page 14, A7 of the Committee's First Report and page 35, A14 of its Ninth Report of last session, it would be helpful to have a note on the use of the TACEVAL system to develop measures of capability and readiness.

A2. TACEVAL—Capability and readiness

The aim of Tactical Evaluation (TACEVAL) is to assess for Supreme Allied Commander Europe against prescribed standards the operational capability of NATO Command, Assigned, Earmarked and other NATO Forces, to rate against common standards, to indicate deficiencies and to make recommendations.

The standards, operational capability requirements and performance criteria are set down in Allied Command Europe (ACE) Forces Standards (AFS), whose aim is to establish a common foundation for operational training in peace and employment of air units allocated to ACE during crisis and war.

Evaluations normally cover the following three areas:

****

Although the foregoing relates specifically to NATO allocated units, it is used by HQ RAF Strike Command (STC) as the basis for National TACEVALs within STC. The need to undergo a formal TACEVAL every 24 months provides a focus for a unit's training and exercise programme and is in itself, a very useful measure of a unit's capability and readiness.

Q3. A full list of frequency of live weapons firings would be helpful (Qq 1357–8); and a note on the RAF's aviation fuel allocation system (Q 1359).

A3. Live Firings

A summary of Air-to-Air Missile (AAM) and bomb allocations for live firing exercises in peacetime is as follows:

(a) **** for Strike Attack (SA)/Offensive Support (OS) force practice firings:
    (i) Tornado GR1—****

    (ii) Harrier—****

    (iii) Jaguar—****

This broadly equates to one sidewinder firing per pilot/crew per two tours.

(b) *1,000lb bombs* for practice release:

    (i) Tornado GRT—**** High Explosives (HE) & **** inerts per crew per annum.

    (ii) Harrier—**** HE & **** inerts per pilot per annum.

    (iii) Jaguar—**** HE & **** inerts per pilot per annum.

(c) *AAMs* for Air Defence force practice firings:

    (i) Skyflash—**** per squadron per annum.

    (ii) Sidewinder—**** per squadron per annum.

This broadly equates to one Skyflash and one Sidewinder per crew per tour.

(d) *Ammunition* allocation per pilot/crew per annum is as follows:

    (i) Tornado GR1—**** HE & **** rounds practice.

    (ii) Harrier—**** HE & **** practice.

    (iii) Jaguar—**** HE & **** practice.

    (iv) Tornado F3—**** rounds practice.

(e) *Practice Bombs* allocations for SA/OS forces are as follows:

    (i) Tornado GR1—**** –3kg retard/**** –14kg ballistic.

    (ii) Harrier—**** retard & **** ballistic.

(iii) Jaguar—**** retard & **** ballistic.

On average SA/OS crews will fly three sorties per week and, weather permitting, they will normally try to get into a bombing range on each sortie. However, on the majority of occasions they will only have sufficient fuel and range time to drop one weapon from a First Run Attack profile. At least one sortie per week on average will involve "academic" weapon training in a dedicated 15 minute range slot—sufficient time in normal circumstances to drop four bombs or to carry out six strafe passes.

Aviation Fuel for Operational Conversion Units (OCUs)

The allocation of fuel for OCUs is based on the hours agreed for the training task as decided by the Task Chart Review Committee. The training task takes account of student throughput, training standards and Instructor currency. The agreed hours are divided by the number of established aircraft on the unit to derive a Forecast Flying Rate (FFR) which is the parameter used to provision the fuel. A tasked fuel allocation is reached by multiplying the FFR by the current standard fuel burn rate for the relevant aircraft type.

Aviation Fuel for Frontline Squadrons

The allocation of fuel for Frontline Squadrons is based on a Crew Flying Task (CFT), plus Station Executive Flying which produces an FFR for each aircraft type and unit. (CFT sets a specific hours/crew for each crew to maintain currency; this includes training and operational elements.) The FFR is multiplied by the current standard fuel burn rate for the relevant aircraft type, to produce a tasked fuel allocation.

Q4. It would be helpful to have notes on the outcome of the move of Aircrew Selection from Biggin Hill to Cranwell; on the drop-out rate for aircrew between ITT and IPS; and on the current and projected future proportions of aircrew as between jet, rotary and multi-engine.

A4. The move to Biggin Hill

The relocation of the Officer and Aircrew Selection Centre (OASC) from Biggin Hill to RAF Cranwell took place as planned in August 1992 and candidate selection commenced at Cranwell the following month. A Post Project Evaluation (PPE) has recently been conducted to asses the actual costs and savings involved in the relocation exercise. The results of the PPE demonstrate that despite a significant reduction in the value of the Biggin Hill estate and increases in the new build costs at Cranwell, relocation has proved to be cost-effective and should break even in FY 96–97, only two years later than assumed in the original study.

DROP-OUT BETWEEN INTO TRAINING TARGET (ITT) AND INTO PRODUCTIVE SERVICE (IPS)
Forecast Pilot Training Wastage Rates

The ITT is dictated by the number of Fast Jet Pilots required by frontline squadrons. Of the 192 students who enter into Flying Training, approximately 140 will reach squadron service (an overall wastage rate of 27 per cent).

The historic wastage rates for pilots at each stage of training are shown below:

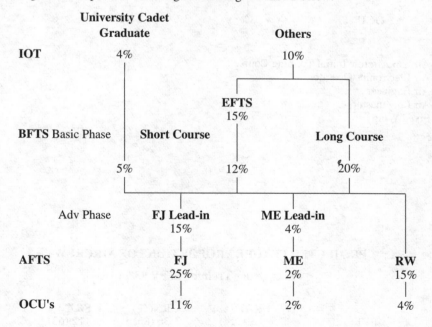

Notes:

IOT —Initial Officer Training	AFTS—Advanced Flying Training School
EFTS—Elementary Flying Training Squadron	OCU —Operational Conversion Unit
BFTS—Basic Flying Training School	RW —Rotary Wing
FJ —Fast Jet	ME —Multi-Engine

FORECAST NAVIGATOR TRAINING WASTAGE RATES

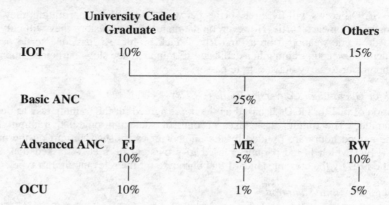

	University Cadet Graduate		Others
IOT	10%		15%
Basic ANC		25%	
Advanced ANC	FJ	ME	RW
	10%	5%	10%
OCU	10%	1%	5%

Notes:
ANC—Air Navigation Course.

FORECAST AIRMEN AIRCREW TRAINING WASTAGE RATES

AAITC	AEOp	Air Eng	ALM	
	10%	9%	5%	
Basic Training	5%	12%	2%	
			ALM FW	ALM RW
Advanced Training	11%		0%	4%
OCU	3%	3%	3%	0%

Notes:
AAITC—Airman Aircrew Initial Training Course
AEOp —Air Electronics Operator
Air Eng—Air Engineer
ALM   —Air Loadmaster
FW   —Fixed Wing

PROJECTED FUTURE PROPORTIONS OF AIRCREW

Pilots Under Training in FY 93/94

	RAF (%)	RN(%)	F&C (%)
EFT	59 (24)	36 (86)	12 (63)
BFT	82 (33)	3 (7)	5 (26)
FJAFT	56 (22)	3 (7)	2 (11)
MEAFT	28 (11)	0 (0)	0 (0)
RWAFT	25 (10)	0 (0)	0 (0)
Total	250 (100)	42 (100)	19 (100)

Navigators Under Training in FY 93–94

	RAF (%)	F&C (%)
BNC	47 (47)	3 (100)
FJANC	20 (20)	0 (0)
MEANC	10 (10)	0 (0)
RWANC	23 (23)	0 (0)
TOTAL	100 (100)	3 (100)

Planned Pilot IPS Targets

	FY 94–95 (%)	FY 95–96 (%)	FY 96–97 (%)
FJ	33 (35)	40 (33)	40 (33)
ME	35 (38)	50 (41)	47 (38)
RW	17 (18)	22 (18)	26 (21)
CFS	8 (9)	10 (8)	10 (8)
TOTAL	93 (100)	122 (100)	123 (100)

Notes:
CFS—Central Flying School

Planned Navigator IPS Targets

	FY 94–95 (%)	FY 95–96 (%)	FY 96–97 (%)
FJ	15 (34)	16 (40)	18 (43)
ME	15 (34)	15 (38)	15 (36)
RW	14 (32)	9 (22)	9 (21)
TOTAL	44 (100)	40 (100)	42 (100)

Q5. It would be helpful to have details of the changed costing criteria for training referred to at Q1330, and its impact on offering training spaces to overseas crews.

A5. Costing Criteria

The Chief Executive of the Training Group Defence Agency has introduced the concept of business development in order to maximise income by marketing unavoidable spare capacity, and to identify opportunities to use existing assets to generate additional revenue. A Business Development Office has been created to coordinate the Agency's business development activities. All repayment service work will continues to be undertaken in accordance with Departmental and Treasury guidelines. The Chief Executive is seeking the freedom to negotiate the prices charged for the Agency's services and to charge what the markets will bear.

11.   Memorandum submitted by the Ministry of Defence on the outcome of the Command and Staff Training Study (8 July 1993)

Q1. The Committee considered the Department's consultative document on RN Engineer Officer Training etc, and noted the reference in paragraph 2 to the Armed Forces Command and Staff (CST) Study. It has asked for details of the outcome of this study.

A1(i) The Ministry of Defence has been considering the future arrangements for Command and Staff Training (CST). The courses involved are those provided by the single Service Staff Colleges (at Greenwich, Camberley and Bracknell for the Royal Navy, Army and Royal Air Force respectively, with the Army and RAF also running certain junior level courses, the Junior Command and Staff Course (JCSC) and the Officers Command Course (OCC), at Warminster and Henlow respectively) and the Joint Service Defence College, which is also at Greenwich. The work initially involved examining the costs and feasibility of collocating some or all of the courses concerned at Greenwich, Camberley or Bracknell. (A further option, to use a combination of the Camberley and Bracknell sites, which are relatively close to each other, was ruled out early in the work, because it was evident that the savings in running costs and from estate disposals would have been more modest than those expected from single site options.)

(ii) Our costing work revealed that all these options would produce savings over a 20 year period, but that the scale of the savings would be modest in relation to the initial capital investment required; the details are at Annex A. It has been decided therefore not to proceed with the collocation of CST on an inter-Service basis.

(iii) It is clear, though, that as a consequence of the impact in the support area of "Defence for the 90s", there is scope for achieving some economies in this area of training. The details are as follows.

(iv) *Royal Navy.* The Royal Navy already benefit from the collocation of junior and advanced staff training (the RN Initial Staff Course and the RN Staff Course respectively) at Greenwich, and from the presence there also of a small civilian academic lecturing staff (the Department of History and International Affairs), which provides second degree accreditation with the University of London. No significant changes are therefore currently proposed to the arrangements for providing all levels of RN CST at Greenwich and the scope for major savings in the future is limited, although appropriate economies will continue to be made where possible.

(v) *Army.* The Army are planning to move the JCSC from Warminster to the Camberley/Sandhurst complex. This will allow the concentration of all core Army officer training courses on one site, with the exception of technical courses, which will continue to be provided at the Royal Military College of Science (RMCS) at Shrivenham. The JCSC will cease functioning at Warminster by this August and restart at Camberley in January 1994. The accommodation released by this move will be used by the Infantry Support Weapons Wing, which will relocate from Netheravon, and the Royal Armoured Corps Tactics Wing, which will relocate from Bovington. This continues to centralisation and rationalisation of tactical training at the Combined Arms Training Centre at Warminster.

(vi) *RAF.* The RAF are planning, along the lines of RMCS Shrivenham, to establish a partnership with an academic "provider", who will take over from RAF personnel responsibility for teaching some 30 per cent of the RAF Advanced Staff Course and at least 50 per cent of the junior level RAF CST courses. The provider will be selected competitively later this year from a range of academic institutions who are showing an interest. Further savings will result from the restructuring and modularisation of the junior level courses, with a much greater emphasis than now on providing the training when needed by the individual (rather than as part of an automatic progression through courses) and on the use of distance learning and short residential training periods.

(vii) The Army and RAF measures combined will save some £15.2 million in net present value terms over 20 years, for set up costs of £12.6 million cash, of which £3.5 million on works at Camberley would need to be spent anyway in any option which involved retention of Camberley. These figures compare favourably with those shown in the Annex.

ANNEX A

SUMMARY OF COSTINGS

£000s

Set Up Costs (Cash)	20 Year Savings (Net Present Value)

A. *Tri-Service Collocation at Camberley, including Joint Service Defence College*

31,160	17,106

B. *Tri-Service Collocation at Camberley, including Joint Service Defence College, Junior Command and Staff Course and Officer Command Course*

33,743	14,736

C. *Tri-Service Collocation at Bracknell, including Joint Service Defence College*

22,026	16,015

D. *Tri-Service Collocation at Bracknell, including Joint Service Defence College, Junior Command and Staff Course and Officer Command Course*

27,479	12,493

E. *Army and RAF Collocation at Camberley, including Junior Command and Staff Course and Officer Command Course; RN and Joint Service Defence College remain at Greenwich*

18,060	6,743

F. *Army and RAF Collocation at Camberley, including Junior Command and Staff Course and Officer Command Course; RN and Joint Service Defence College remain at Greenwich*

10,700	2,232

G. *Tri-Service Collocation at Greenwich, including Joint Service Defence College*

25,450	13,988

ISBN 0-10-209394-6

9 780102 093940